Penn Greek Drama Series

Series Editors
David R. Slavitt
Palmer Bovie

The Penn Greek Drama Series presents fresh literary translations of the entire corpus of classical Greek drama: tragedies, comedies, and satyr plays. The only contemporary series of all the surviving work of Aeschylus, Sophocles, Euripides, Aristophanes, and Menander, this collection brings together men and women of literary distinction whose versions of the plays in contemporary English poetry can be acted on the stage or in the individual reader's theater of the mind.

The aim of the series is to make this cultural treasure accessible, restoring as faithfully as possible the original luster of the plays and offering in living verse a view of what talented contemporary poets have seen in their readings of these works so fundamental a part of Western civilization.

Aeschylus, 2

The Persians, Seven Against Thebes,
The Suppliants, Prometheus Bound

Edited by
David R. Slavitt *and* Palmer Bovie

PENN

University of Pennsylvania Press
Philadelphia

This volume is for Bernard Knox and in Memory of William Matthews

Copyright © 1999 University of Pennsylvania Press
Printed in the United States of America on acid-free paper

10 9 8 7 6 5 4 3 2 1

Published by
University of Pennsylvania Press
Philadelphia, Pennsylvania 19104-4011

Library of Congress Cataloging-in-Publication Data
Aeschylus.
[Works. English. 1998]
Aeschylus / edited by David R. Slavitt and Palmer Bovie
    p.   cm. — (Penn Greek drama series)
Contents: 1. The Oresteia.—2. The Persians, Seven Against Thebes, The Suppliants, Prometheus Bound.
ISBN 0-8122-3416-2 (v. 1 : acid free paper). — ISBN 0-8122-1627-X (pbk : v. 1 : acid free paper). — ISBN 0-8122-3465-0 (v. 2: acid free paper).
ISBN 0-8122-1671-7 (pbk.: v. 2 : acid free paper).
1. Aeschylus—Translations into English.   2. Greek drama (Tragedy)—Translations into English.   3. Mythology, Greek—Drama.   I. Slavitt, David R., 1935–   .   II. Bovie, Smith Palmer.   III. Title.   IV. Series.
PA3827.A657   1997
882'.01—dc21   97-28894
                                                                              CIP

Contents

Introduction

Palmer Bovie

Classical Greek tragedy, which flourished in Athens during the fifth century B.C., grew out of country festivals originating a century earlier. Three different celebrations in honor of Dionysus, known as the rural Dionysia, occurred during the winter months. One of these, the Lenaea, was also observed at Athens in the sanctuary of Dionysus. In addition to song it offered ecstatic dances and comedy. Another, the Anthesteria, lasted for three days as a carnival time of revelry and wine drinking. It also included a remembrance of the dead and was believed to be connected with Orestes' mythical return to Athens purged of guilt for killing his mother Clytemnestra.

The rural Dionysia were communal holidays observed to honor Dionysus, the god of wine, of growth and fertility, and of lightning. Free-spirited processions to an altar of Dionysus were crowned by lyrical odes to the god sung by large choruses of men and boys chanting responsively under the direction of their leader. The ritual included the sacrifice of a goat at the god's altar, from which the term "tragedy," meaning goat-song, may derive. Gradually themes of a more serious nature gained ground over the joyful, exuberant addresses to the liberating god, legends of familiar heroes, and mythological tales of divine retribution. But the undercurrent of the driving Dionysiac spirit was seldom absent, even in the sophisticated artistry of the masterful tragic poets of the fifth century.

Initially the musical texts were antiphonal exchanges between the chorus and its leader. Thespis, who won the prize of a goat for tragedy at Athens in 534 B.C., is traditionally said to have been the first to appear as an actor, separate from the chorus, speaking a prologue and making set speeches, with his face variously disguised by a linen mask. A fourth festival, the City Dionysia or the Great Dionysia, was instituted by the ruler Peisistratus, also in 534, and nine years later Aeschylus was born. It seems that the major era of Greek tragic art was destined to begin.

The Great Dionysia, an annual occasion for dramatic competitions in tragedy and comedy, was held in honor of Dionysus Eleutheros. Its five-day celebration began with a procession in which the statue of Dionysus was carried to the nearby village of Eleutherai (the site of the Eleusinian Mysteries) and then back, in a parade by torchlight, to Athens and the precincts of Dionysus on the lower slopes of the Acropolis. In the processional ranks were city officials, young men of military age leading a bull, foreign residents of Athens wearing scarlet robes, and participants in the dramatic contests, including the producers (*choregoi*), resplendent in colorful costumes. The ceremonies ended with the sacrificial slaughter of the bull and the installation of Dionysus' statue on his altar at the center of the orchestra.

For three days each of the poets chosen for the competition presented his work, three tragedies and one satyr play (a farcical comedy performed in the afternoon after an interval following the staging of tragedies). In the late afternoon comedies were offered. The other two days were marked by dithyrambic competitions, five boys' choruses on one day, five men's on the other. The dithyramb, earlier an excited dramatic dance, became in the Athenian phase a quieter performance, sung by a chorus of fifty and offering little movement.

The theater of Dionysus at Athens was an outdoor space on the southern slope of the Acropolis. A semicircular auditorium was created on the hillside from stone or marble slabs, or shaped from the natural rock with wooden seats added. Narrow stepways gave access to the seats, the front row of which could be fitted out with marble chairs for official or distinguished members of the audience. From sites visible today at Athens, Delphi, Epidaurus, and elsewhere, it is evident that the sloping amphitheater had excellent acoustic properties and that the voices of the actors and the chorus were readily heard.

The acting area began with an *orchestra*, a circular space some sixty feet in diameter where the chorus performed its dance movements, voiced its commentaries, and engaged in dialogue with the actors. In the center of the orchestra was an altar of Dionysus, and on it a statue of the god. Behind the orchestra several steps led to a stage platform in front of the *skene*, a wooden building with a central door and doors at each end and a flat roof. The actors could enter and exit through these doors or one of the sides, retiring to assume different masks and costumes for a change of role. They could also appear on the roof for special effects, as in Euripides' *Orestes* where at the end Orestes and Pylades appear, menacing Helen with death, before she is whisked away from them by Apollo. The skene's facade represented a palace or temple and could have an altar in front of it. Stage properties included the *eccyclema*, a wheeled platform that was rolled out from the central door or the side of the skene to display an interior setting or a tableau, as at the end of Aeschylus' *Agamemnon* where the murdered bodies of Agamemnon and Cassandra are proudly displayed by Clytemnestra.

Another piece of equipment occasionally brought into play was the *mechane*, a tall crane that could lift an actor or heavy objects (e.g., Medea in her chariot) high above the principals' heads. This device, also known as the *deus ex machina*, was favored by Euripides, who in the climactic scene of *Orestes* shows Apollo protecting Helen in the air high above Orestes and Pylades on the roof. Or a deity may appear above the stage to resolve a final conflict and bring the plot to a successful conclusion, as the figure of Athena does at the end of Euripides' *Iphigenia in Tauris*. Sections of background at each end of the stage could be revolved to indicate a change of scene. These *periaktoi*, triangular in shape, could be shown to the audience to indicate a change of place or, together with thunder and lightning machines, could announce the appearance of a god.

The actors wore masks that characterized their roles and could be changed offstage to allow one person to play several different parts in the same drama. In the earliest period tragedy was performed by only one actor in counterpoint with the chorus, as could be managed, for example, in Aeschylus' *Suppliants*. But Aeschylus himself introduced the role of a second actor, simultaneously present on the stage, Sophocles made use of a third, and he and Euripides probably a fourth. From such simple elements (the orchestra space for the chorus, the slightly raised stage and its scene front, the minimal cast of actors) was created the astonishingly powerful poetic drama of the fifth-century Athenian poets.

What we can read and see today is but a small fraction of the work produced by the three major poets and a host of fellow artists who presented plays in the dramatic competitions. Texts of tragedies of Aeschylus, Sophocles, and Euripides were copied and stored in public archives at Athens, along with Aristophanes' comedies. At some later point a selection was made of the surviving plays, seven by Aeschylus, seven by Sophocles, nine by Euripides, and ten others of his discovered by chance. In the late third and early second centuries B.C., this collection of thirty-three plays was conveyed to the great library of Alexandria, where scholarly commentaries, *scholia*, formed part of the canon, to be copied and transmitted to students and readers in the Greco-Roman cultural world.

Aeschylus (525–456 B.C.) was born of a noble Athenian family and lived during the early days of the city's democratic glory. Indeed, Pericles was the *choregus* (producer) of his *Persians* in 472. Aeschylus was an honored, public-spirited citizen who fought in the infantry ranks at the battle of Marathon in 490 and ten years later at Salamis in the victorious struggles against the Persian invasions. His magnificent poetic style established the standard structure of high tragedy. There is the prologue, the opening chorus, the entrance of the actors, who engage in dialogue with their antagonists, with sympathetic friends, or with the chorus. The five or six episodes that constitute the narrative of the play's action are distinguished from one another by choral odes that reflect on the dilemmas arising from the plot or voice lyrical accounts of comparable situations known from myth or history.

The poetry does not refrain from vivid descriptions of death and disaster, but the actual scenes of violence occur offstage and are customarily reported by messengers entering with the shocking news. Greek tragedy, in general, is not the exploitation of human misfortune. It is, rather, a serious inquiry into moral problems, and at the outset Aeschylus equips his players and their choral spectators with challenging ideas. Revenge and retributive justice are misleading paths: "only the act of evil breeds others to follow"; "wisdom comes alone through suffering." Ares, the god of war, is the money changer of dead bodies who packs smooth urns with ashes that once were men: we are given such thoughts to ponder in the *Agamemnon*, but in the last play of this trilogy the court of the Areopagus frees Orestes of the guilt he incurred, with Electra's complicity, for matricide, and distributive justice prevails over an endless cycle of retaliation.

Prometheus the Titan, in *Prometheus Bound* chained in torment to a mountain rock for having brought the gift of fire to mortals and with it the basis of civilized progress, realizes that he has given mankind "blind hopes"; he admits that art (*techne*) is far weaker than necessity, human craft bound as it is by its own mortal limits. But, as the two next plays in that trilogy suggest in their titles, *Prometheus Unbound* and *Prometheus the Firebearer*, his story ends in a triumphant reconciliation with Zeus, whose tyrannical pride has learned to replace selfish elusiveness with an understanding of humankind's capability and right to improve their own condition.

Hermes, the messenger of Zeus in this cosmic drama, mocks Prometheus for having defied Zeus' authority and for being proud of enabling people to rise above their animal instincts and apply the use of reason. But, since Prometheus is to be released from bondage to the supreme ruler of the universe and ultimately recognized proudly (!) for giving mortals the means, the technology, for progress, the tragic ordeal becomes a triumph of good judgment. As George Orwell once wrote, somewhat bleakly, on the same subject: "Progress is not an illusion; but it is gradual and inevitably disappointing." [1]

Aeschylus' imagination ranges over the known world. His "suppliants," the fifty innocent Danaids, escape from Egypt and from their Egyptian cousins who are menacing them with forced marriage, to Argos in Greece, where they gain the protection of the king, Pelasgus. The setting of *The Persians* is Susa, the residence of the Persian kings. Its characters include Atossa, the Queen Mother, and the ghost of Darius, and Xerxes, stripped of his pride. The drama is the only historical member of the canon, with its colorful description of the battle of Salamis and its poignant portrayal of an enemy in defeat. *Seven Against Thebes* extends the revenge saga of the ruling dynasty of this city-state, even as it illustrates the utter futility of war.

Prometheus Bound is a cosmic pageant and a chance for Aeschylus to revel in his knowledge of geography. The wanderings of Io, foreseen by Prometheus (whose name means "forethought"), describe the Near East, starting from the southern Caucasus and proceeding southward along the entire Ionian coast, to end in Egypt. In the course of this excursion through exotic place names, Aeschylus trained one sly glance on a river he himself invented. Prometheus warns Io not to cross the river Hybristes, the River Insolence. It tends to overflow its banks. One cannot locate this river on a map, but the idea sticks in one's mind. The whole drama is on a huge scale, its cast composed exclusively of immortals. We see Hephaestus and the huge figures Power and Violence who hustle in as the play opens to bind

---

1. Orwell, "Politics and the English Language, " *New Republic*, 1947; reprinted in various collections.

the Titan to his mountain rock. He is visited and interviewed there by the Oceanids (who form the chorus) and their father Oceanus, then by Io who in her harassed state of prolonged wandering from Greece to Egypt will continue to be as tormented in her perpetual motion as Prometheus is tortured in his fixed bondage to the vindictive plans of Zeus. When Hermes arrives to try to talk Prometheus down and persuade him to compromise by divulging his secret knowledge of Zeus' future, Prometheus remains adamant in his defiance of tyrannical power. Their dialogue becomes a snarling duel of wits, as Hermes' tempting rationalizations try to offset Prometheus' naked truths. The play began with Prometheus being chained under the orders of Hephaestus, the god of fire, whose element he has dared to trespass upon. It ends with an earthquake and whirlwind that split the rock on which the hero has been impaled and hurl him into the abyss of Tartarus to endure further torment. An immortal cannot escape punishment by dying. We have witnessed the spectacle of sublime injustice. But from the further stages of the story as planned by Aeschylus it is apparent that the Titan, the benefactor of progress to mortals, outlasted his agonizing ordeal to become the object of mortals' grateful veneration.

The imagery and metaphorical insights of Aeschylus' verse range through a spectrum of associations. The Oceanids view Prometheus through "a mist of tears and fears"; they see him held "in bonds of adamantine shame." His words are sharpened swords. Fire is Hephaestus' flower, its flame a curling tendril. The want of good sense in Zeus has tangled him in a net of ruin. In *The Oresteia*, Agamemnon's return is to "my palace for which I have so long yearned." Similar irony attends the chorus' description of him as a lion-king who leaped over the walls of Troy and lapped the blood of kings. Helen, whose name is cognate with the verb "to destroy," is Troy's "bride and bane." She is like a lion cub that grows up to develop claws and ferocity. Iphigenia is the innocent lamb of sacrifice. In ambiguous pleasure, Clytemnestra greets her husband's homecoming with "griefless heart," comparing him to "that brook from which [the parched and weakened traveler] can drink sweet water." She will be glad to slake her thirst.

In her turn, Electra says: "Even the dead can hope. Drowned men can rise / like corks in the sea, / and corpses ascend from their graves to thrive / and prosper in air, in their heirs who are yet alive."

In *The Eumenides* imagery is overshadowed by the strenuous rhetoric of argument, as the Furies lash out at Apollo and Athena, who engineer Orestes' acquittal and his trial before a jury of twelve (the first in Athenian history). The drama explores Orestes' degree of responsibility for his wrong-doing and advances the idea that moral problems can be suitably addressed by the powers of human understanding. Crime is not something to be furious about but rather a complex social concern to be curious about. The spirit of vengeance symbolized by the Furies merely reinforces the human condition as the plight of a compulsive, aggressive creature. In effecting Orestes' redemption from sin Athena also works a magical transformation in the image of the Erinyes, the Furies, who are persuaded to assume a new role as the Eumenides, kindly spirits. They will reside in Athens as guardian spirits, gladly responsible for the protection of social justice among its citizens. The surprising transformation fulfills the hope expressed much earlier in the trilogy by a choral refrain in the *Agamemnon*:

We sing a dirge but hope that good may prevail.

The Persians

Translated by
David R. Slavitt

Translator's Preface

It is perhaps presumptuous of me to offer an introduction to a play into which I have obtruded a Prologue who speaks, I freely admit, on my behalf throughout the performance. But it is appealing to take this opportunity to repay him and speak on his behalf. At the very least, I can vouch for what he says about how, in Attic Greek, important place names are preceded by an article. (I remember the classroom example: "The Boston," or even "The Cambridge," but just plain "Somerville.") Kings also get an article, except for the king of Persia, for whom that deliberate omission and its disrespect amount to a grammatical rule. You can look it up in Goodwin's *Greek Grammar*.

Such hatred may look these days to be politically incorrect. We mustn't hold the Germans collectively responsible for the Shoah. We can't blame all the Japanese for Pearl Harbor and the rape of Nanking. We're not supposed to generalize about any ethnicities because it isn't nice.

Aeschylus wouldn't have understood any of that. (Neither, indeed, would Cavafy, whose poems make it clear that there are Greeks and then there are the barbarians, which is to say, the rest of the world.) To Aeschylus, hatred was a perfectly reasonable human emotion, and to attempt to deny it would have been to deny the truth of one's own experience. His epitaph, which Plutarch tells us he composed for himself, makes no mention of his career as a playwright but says simply, "Here lies Aeschylus, son of Euphorion, whose valor at Marathon the Long-haired Persians may remember."

The Persians was produced in Athens in 472 B.C., eight years after the defeat of Xerxes at the battle of Salamis. Pericles put up the money for the production, which was a celebration of that defeat and a monument to it. It is a tragedy only by the furthest stretching of the rules. But then Aeschylus didn't have to worry about Aristotle's rules because they hadn't been written yet: in fact, he was one of those who were making them up. This isn't any account of the downfall of a hero through some tragic flaw; there are no pity and terror here; and there is no catharsis. What we have, instead, is the Athenians' exultation in the recent ruin of their real enemies.

I reread *The Persians* some years ago in order to try to clarify my thoughts about W. D. Snodgrass' *The Fuehrer Bunker*,[1] a difficult and troubling poem about Hitler, Goebbels, Goering, Eva Braun, and that crew in the bunker in Berlin in 1945. It is a sordid and obscene but fascinating piece. Here, for instance, is a bit of Goebbels:

> I am that spirit that denies,
> High Priest of Laymen, Prince of Lies.
> Your house is founded on my rock:
> Truth crows; now I deny my cock.
> Jock of this walk, I turn down all,
> Robbing my Peter to play Paul.
>
> I give up all goods I possess
> To build my faith on faithlessness.
> Black Peter, I belie my Lord—
> You've got to die to spread the Word.
> Now the last act; there's no sequel.
> Soon, once more, all things shall be equal. (p. 116)

How is one to take such a display of brilliant nastiness? The answer is in this, the oldest of the surviving Greek plays. We are to delight in the ruin of our enemies, the Persians, and to exult in their anguish.

To fail to do so is to miss the point. But that, indeed, is how some people have been reading the text. Seth Benardete declares in the introduction to his rendition, "To show sympathetically, *sine ira et studio*, on the stage at Athens the defeat of her deadliest enemy testifies to the humanity of Aeschylus and the Athenians. No other tragedian we know of, of any country at any time, has ever dared to go so far in sympathizing with his country's foe. It is the more remarkable when we consider that Aeschylus himself and almost all his audience fought at Salamis or Plataea and that the war, moreover, was between freedom and slavery."[2]

My view is altogether different. I can't imagine Aeschylus believing any of that liberal claptrap for a minute. On the contrary, I see his play as working in just the way Snodgrass' extraordinary poem does. And my attempt

---

[1] Brockport, N.Y.: BOA Editions, 1995.
[2] Chicago: University of Chicago Press, 1956.

here is to make clear that this is a display of *Schadenfreude*, an elegant cocking of the snooks, a protracted "Na-na, na-na, boo-boo," a symphonic Bronx cheer!

My Prologue is an intrusion, a tour guide, if you will. But the rest of the play is as close as I could come to the text—and, I believe, the spirit—of the Greek original.

Edward Said complains in his *Orientalism* that Europeans have always looked down on Orientals and thought of them as cruel, sybaritic barbarians who are not quite human. And he's quite right. The question he avoids, however, is whether this harsh characterization is incorrect or unfair. Persia—or, now, Iran—is a fundamentalist state that sponsors terrorism and issues fatwahs against those of whom it disapproves. Lacking in restraint and respect for law, this is a nation that, in Aeschylus' view, forfeits the right to be taken seriously.

If European history is mostly a long St. Bartholomew's Day, with the Inquisition, the Terror, the Holocaust, and, more recently, the Bosnians and the Serbs and their ethnic cleansings, there have been at least the occasional professions, mostly honored in the breach, of the dignity of man and the authority of God.

But brotherhood of man? That is something else and, after Cain and Abel, not very much of a claim. And I am as sure as I can be that "I'd like to buy the world a Coke" was not the message of Aeschylus' play.

If I'm wrong? I haven't destroyed the Greek text but only rendered it. I've given my reading of the play I think Aeschylus probably wrote.

Now that a papyrus fragment has revised the dating of the *Supplices*, *The Persians* takes its place as the earliest surviving Greek play, the *fons et origo* of this amazing body of work. It was also the first play to be translated in what became the Penn series. Having arrived through the Snodgrass poem at the wonderfully spiteful energy of this play, I thought this vision of the piece was worth sharing. And this one play was all I intended, at least at first, to do. That notion was the flutter of the butterfly wing in Siberia that produces, somehow, a typhoon in the South Pacific, or, in this case, the Penn Greek Drama Series.

I am proud of the series that Palmer Bovie, Eric Halpern, and I have been able to put together. It turns out, I think, to be just the right setting for this extraordinary piece, which remains, in its way, my favorite.

Cast

CHORUS OF PERSIAN ELDERS
PROLOGUE
QUEEN OF PERSIA
HERALD
GHOST OF DARIUS, king of Persia
XERXES, son of Darius

*(A bare stage. A fanfare and then a slow drum beat. A Chorus of
Persian Elders files on stage. They are whispering to one another.
From the other side, a Prologue enters, watches them, looks out
into the auditorium, shakes his head as if in disbelief—or is it
disapproval?—and then, as the drum beats fade away, addresses
the audience directly.)*

PROLOGUE
    The chorus of Persian elders files in,
    the enemy we despise. As if
    performing for us, pretending we do not
    watch them and hear them speak those words
    we love to hear, they converse like normal
    people who reassure one another,
    helpful, kindly, or merely polite,
    that the news they will soon receive of the battle
    may cause their rejoicing or let them at least
    relax, worried as any civilians   10
    must be for their friends and sons in the army.
    Dead, all dead now, hacked into pieces,
    maimed and their armor ripped from their bleeding
    bodies before their eyes went dull.
    But these people have no idea.
    Consider them in this lovely moment
    of a decade ago. They are stuck forever

and the news is always about to arrive.
Ignorance endlessly ended, like innocence
ravished again and again, while we   20
watch. There must always be one Greek
somewhere in the seats, for without him,
nothing we see here makes any sense.
They will cry out in their deep anguish
that through his eyes is delightful and sweet;
they will beat their breasts and weep,
but to his ears their cries will be music.
He is the play, that man beside you.
Watch him, off to your left or right,
and consider his smile, that satisfied rictus   30
at the Persian's defeat and shame and heartbreak.

   He may well notice that you have been glancing
in his direction, but do not worry
for this will please him. You will be
a part of the play he watches. Your
attention will add an exotic flavor,
will garnish his joy in this re-enactment.
He loves to be seen attending *The Persians*
and watching them, who are quite unaware.
He is Athenian; he can assume   40
that you, a New Yorker or Californian,
will envy him, as you note his special
delight in which you cannot share,
except, of course, by a substitution
from time to time for the word "Persians"
translating that to "Japanese"
or "Confederate," or, as the French would call them,
"Germans" (and Russians would call them "French").

   They are the others, the orientals,
the Asiatics, strange and cruel,   50
"civilized" but not altogether,
for that word, if it extends to them,
loses most of its meaning and value.

Our sacred notions of family honor,
justice, and piety, they have defied
and defiled, and they deserve to suffer.
Aeschylus was there. He fought
and left on his gravestone the declaration
that Marathon could speak of his valor
that the long-haired Persians (that was an insult)   60
remembered and they could speak of it too.
To understand is not to forgive.
People do wrong, and countries too,
for which there is only the one relief
of the shedding of blood and bitter tears.
To let go of a deep enough hatred
is to let go your sense of yourself,
to deny the truth of your own life,
and bleat like sheep who forgive the shepherd
wearing the skins of their brothers and fathers.   70
Listen, therefore, but try not to feel
excessive sorrow. Indeed, they suffer
but they have earned what they get and more.
(He moves to the proscenium and directs the audience's attention to the
Chorus.)

FIRST CHORISTER
    We are the elders,
    Persia's caretakers,
    waiting to hear
    the news from the front.

SECOND CHORISTER *(singing, from the Mikado)*
    Miya sama, miya sama, on n'm-ma no mayé ni . . .

FIRST CHORISTER *(trying to ignore the interruption)*
    All Asia has joined the battle,
    Sousa and Agbatana and Kissa . . .   80

THIRD CHORISTER *(shouting)*
  We will bury them!

FIRST CHORISTER *(carrying on as well as he can)*
  On horse and by ship,
  swordsmen and archers,
  the edge of their courage
  whetted and dreadful . . .

SECOND CHORISTER
  A warm water port! A place in the sun!
  A Reich that will last a thousand years!

FIRST CHORISTER
  From Lydia's gentle coast, the kings,
  Metrogathes and brave Arkteus,
  from Cairo and Thebes, with men from the marshes,   90
  the brave commanders and charioteers . . .

THIRD CHORISTER
  To end the tyranny of the imperialist exploitation,
  to establish justice and peace, to let the world know
  we will not be fucked with any more . . .

FIRST CHORISTER *(gives a stern look to the third chorister, then*
                      continues)
  From Tmolus and Sardis,
  from all over Asia,
  tribes have assembled,
  and the flower of Persia
  is gone to fulfill
  that glorious destiny   100
  the gods have awarded us,
  admirals, generals doing the bidding
  of Xerxes, our ruler and King of Kings.

SECOND CHORISTER
    Might, after all, makes right. What the gods
    permit is clearly what they command.
    To suppose otherwise is to hate heaven
    and therefore deserve death's rough correction!
(The first chorister is pleased by the second chorister's display of
                    decorum.)

THIRD CHORISTER *(singing)*
    Hutu, tootsie, don't cry . . .
    Too, too tutsi, goodbye!

FIRST CHORISTER *(exasperated, shuts third chorister up, then resumes)*
    The beds of the wives are damp with tears,   110
    as each waits for her noble lord
    in a torment of longing and apprehension.

THIRD CHORISTER *(not intimidated at all)*
    But they'll be back, laden with booty.
    Those gates will be smashed, those proud towers
    thrown down into the dust . . . The Greeks?
    Olive-oil salesmen! Owners of diners
    and pizza parlors! The men wear skirts
    and their wives and mothers have mustaches!

FIRST CHORISTER *(he has, at this point, more or less given up)*
    Let us pray for Darius' son,
    as we wait here for the news of Xerxes   120
    latest triumph in arrows' rain
    and the hail of spears as he comes like a god
    to impose the will of heaven on earth.

SECOND CHORISTER
    Lebensraum! Mare Nostrum!
    Chechnya for the Chechins! Free
    Quebec! Banzai! Geronimo!

Damn the torpedoes. Kilroy is here!
I only regret I have but the one
life to give for my country's flag!
(They resume their sotto voce conversation among themselves.)

PROLOGUE
A beastly people, but every people   130
is beastly to every other. We hate
whatever is different, and everyone is.
But on this theatrical stage, their boasting
is harmless and therefore entertaining.
We know what waits in the wings. The Queen
is about to appear, and not far behind her,
the Herald with his delightful report
of an utterly lovely and total disaster.
The bolt of lightning has already flashed.
Counting seconds, we wait for the thunder.   140
(Queen enters.)

CHORUS *(ensemble)*
Lo! she comes, the Queen of Persia,
Xerxes' aged mother, the great
Darius' consort, the nation's mistress.
How bravely she bears our country's cares,
how stately her walk, how clear her gaze
as she sets us all a fine example,
confident that good news will come
of her son's success and her people's triumph!

FIRST CHORISTER
O great lady! We, your counselors
attending you here, proffer our love   150
and service, however we can, as your guides,
but you are the one from whom we take
our strength and our inadequate wisdom.

QUEEN

> I come from the golden palace to raise
> the people's spirits, or rather, say
> I help to maintain them. Rich displays
> dazzle the eyes and soothe the spirit,
> for this expensive paraphernalia
> shows how the gods have looked with favor
> on Darius' house and Xerxes' kingship.   160
> Those whom the gods love must trust them
> fearing nothing and no one. Wealth
> can turn a person or even a country
> cautious and soft, but the dictates of prudence
> can only arise from doubt in the gods'
> dependability and their love.

(Prologue raises his arms, and the Queen and the Chorus freeze.)

PROLOGUE

> Isn't it lovely? What could we think of
> better for her to say and believe
> than just such nonsense. We must allow them
> a little humanity, even some sense,   170
> in order for them to comprehend
> their loss. We must assume they feel,
> as keenly as we do, the pain of bereavement.

(He lowers his arms. The Queen resumes.)

QUEEN

> What Darius made, Xerxes enlarges,
> for his son Artaxerxes to nurture
> and further enlarge. The world will be
> Persian—and all the better for it.
> And yet, I am troubled by strange dreams
> of ambiguous portent. Last night's vision
> was of two women, splendidly dressed,   180
> one in the Persian style and one
> in the Doric mode, but beauties both.

Sisters, they were, but quarrelsome sisters,
arguing over which should have what
and who should live where. And then my son
yoked them together as horses or oxen,
bridled their necks, and set them in tandem
to draw his car. One was obliging,
but the other, recalcitrant, would not be managed,
tore off the tracings, and broke the yoke,   190
and my son was thrown by the vehicle's lurching.
Darius, who saw this all, was weeping,
and Xerxes, ashamed at his father's tears,
tore his royal robes in remorse.

FIRST CHORISTER
It's clear enough, but be reassured
these are the fears any mother must feel
and not the omens of gods or fates.

QUEEN (*hardly taking any notice of the chorister*)
I roused myself from this troubled sleep
and went to the spring and the gods' altar
to pray that these voices of doubt and fear   200
prove to be only a mother's fancies, ·
and there, as I turned to Apollo's hearth,
I saw an eagle swooping and soaring,
enjoying the morning, I thought at first,
but I caught sight of the falcon he fled.
It wheeled and dove and its claws seized
the eagle as if it were merely a rabbit
helpless and terrified. I was awake
and therefore all the more afraid.

SECOND CHORISTER
What have the birds to do with us?   210
Men who have failed look to the omens
to find excuses. But those who succeed

create themselves and make their own
destinies as an act of will.

FIRST CHORISTER *(less reckless)*
    Or it may be these are thoughts of the gods
    that need not come to pass. Queen mother,
    approach the altars with offerings, pray
    for your son and your city, invoke the ghost
    of your husband, Darius, who came to your dream
    with kindly comfort. Hidden in darkness,   220
    good and evil compete together.
    Our prayers and faith may tip the balance,
    or so wise men have always supposed.

PROLOGUE *(interrupting the action again)*
    What prognosis can we imagine?
    This is an autopsy! There is the corpse,
    a display of corrupt meat on a slab.
    And still they discuss its hopes and prospects?
    Aristophanes never wrote
    a more hilarious piece.
                 In a moment
    the Herald will come to deliver the news.   230

QUEEN
    I thank you both for your comforting words.
    I shall indeed offer prayers and libations,
    but tell me again, do you think it can happen
    that Xerxes can unite the whole world?

FIRST CHORISTER
    What men can think of, men can do.
    The wealth of the Greeks and the strength they waste
    in warfare among their city-states
    will benefit mankind all the more
    when applied to peaceful uses. Your son

will prescribe for them as a good physician   240
a healthier life. Commerce will thrive,
and the arts and sciences prosper in peace
Darius tried to impose and Xerxes
will surely achieve, to the glory of both
the father and son.

QUEEN

                I trust you are right.
As queen I hope, and as mother I fear,
and I try to endure this burden of waiting . . .

THIRD CHORISTER

Which comes at last to an end, great lady!
I see the Persian runner approach
with his report of how the war goes.   250
(Enter Herald. He bows to the Queen, then comes to attention.)

HERALD

Persia, Cities of Asia, hear me!
My dreadful duty is bringing the news
all at once. It is bitter indeed,
for the battle is lost. We are defeated,
routed, scattered, ruined, undone,
crushed, smashed, savaged, broken,
whipped, bested, beaten, cowed . . .

THIRD CHORISTER

Enough! We take your general meaning.

SECOND CHORISTER

Woe! Alas! Terrible, terrible . . .

FIRST CHORISTER

In a moment, one feels a decade older.   260
Life loses its sweetness and color,
and all is drab and dull as dust.

HERALD

    I was there. I can describe it.
    Worse than anything you can imagine,
    the hulls overturned, the corpses of soldiers
    and sailors like kelp that bobs in the waves
    that surge and recede from the hostile shingle.

SECOND CHORISTER

    Woe! Alas! Terrible, terrible . . .

HERALD

    Worse than you can believe. The battle
    need not have taken place. In a siege,   270
    we were doing well by doing nothing,
    but Xerxes, young and brash, was impatient
    and launched an attack. The winds turned wrong
    and drove our ships aground on the sandbars
    that surround the island . . .

THIRD CHORISTER

                    Terrible, terrible . . .

HERALD

    The name of Salamis puckers the mouth
    with bitterness. Mothers and wives, bereaved,
    will hear those syllables ring in their dreams
    the dissonant peal of a broken bell.

SECOND CHORISTER

    Almost as bad, I can imagine   280
    Athenians celebrating and gloating . . .

QUEEN

    I have kept silent till now, but tell me
    the details our sick spirits demand.
    Who was killed? Who was wounded?
    Or captured? And who if any survived—
    beside yourself.

HERALD
>   O great queen,
> Artembares, the leader of horsemen,
> was crushed by waves that broke on the cliffs.
> Dadakes, the satrap, struck by a spear,
> went overboard and either drowned   290
> or died from the wound. Tenagon,
> the Bactrian hero, is dead, and Lilaeus,
> and Arsames and Argestes also.
> Ardeues, from Egypt, Arkteus,
> and Pharnouchus went down on their ship together.
> Matallus, satrap of Chrysa, died,
> his jet-black beard dripping crimson.
> Arabus, and Artabes, allies
> who came with us to share in glory
> died. Amphisterus, the spearman, Amistris,   300
> and Ariomardus, from Sardis, died.
> Seisames, the Mysian, and brave Tharybdis
> the Lyrnaean master of two hundred fifty
> swift ships is dead. And others,
> many others, more than I name,
> more than a man can list in a tally
> or even imagine, are gone. Gone.

PROLOGUE *(interrupting)*
> He could go on for a long time,
> with that list of names. He could do the entire
> Susa phone book and never fear   310
> our interest or appetite would flag.
> For this, he assumes that Athenian, nodding
> beside you and saying under his breath
> again and again, "More, more,
> you fucking bastards! Give them the names.
> With a Chinese water torture, drive them
> to numbness first and then to madness."
(He allows them to resume the action.)

QUEEN

    Oh, the pain! And the shame of the Persians!
    Each is worse than the other and prompts
    our shrill lament. But tell me, Herald,   320
    what was the number of Greek ships
    that wrested this victory from our mighty
    Persian fleet?

HERALD

              It pains me to say,
    but ours was the stronger force. The Greeks
    had three hundred ten vessels to Xerxes'
    thousand or more. Such an imbalance
    ought to have made us the victors, but gods
    or the fates, or the mere whims of the winds
    redressed the odds and held us off.
    They counter-attacked and whipped us soundly.   330

QUEEN *(not quite taking it in yet)*

    I had thought to hear that Athens was sacked,
    the acropolis merely a mound of rubble,
    and all Greeks now were Persian slaves.

HERALD

    Not so, my lady. I'm sorry to say
    Athens is still standing.

QUEEN

              But . . . how?

HERALD

    We were betrayed. Themistocles
    sent a slave, Sicinnus by name,
    to let Xerxes know that the Greeks
    were about to flee in the dark of night.
    Given the numbers, Xerxes believed him   340

and ordered a Persian attack at dawn.
All our rowers and all our marines
readied themselves, and at first light
we hurled ourselves at the enemy's line . . .
They were waiting for us, there at the narrow
mouth of the bay, on both our flanks,
and, when signal trumpets blared, their armada
converged on us like dogs on a doe.
They ripped us apart . . . Their brazen prows
rammed us broadside, smashing our strakes,   350
staving us in, and leaving us helpless.
On every side we were turning turtle,
and under the upturned hulls, our sailors
strapped to their oars cried out in the darkness
and then were silent. The sea was alive
with corpses. It looked like a school of human
fish caught in a net like so many
mackerel, thrashing, flopping, bloody,
cut open by swords or broken oar blades,
or even filleted. The water was red   360
with Persian flotsam, blood and carnage.
But . . . these are merely words. At the time
the horror was such that the mind went blank.
One looked about with an anesthetic
incomprehension. Only later,
in tiny gobbets that memory retched
would pieces come back, and then in safety
the pain and shame and guilt conflated.

QUEEN
    Oh, alas. Oh, woe!

PROLOGUE
    Shall we pause here a moment? Can it get better?   370
    Aeschylus here is playing to Athens'
    appetite for Persian abasement.
    It was even worse than he wrote in his play.

Xerxes at Salamis could have won
and would have, if he had only been patient.
The Greeks, cut off, would indeed have run
in a matter of days. The attack was absurd,
a risk that the Persians need never have taken.
But the wind turned, they were caught in the narrows
and had to fall back, having lost a few ships,   380
and pride, perhaps, but still the advantage
was Xerxes'. Furious, out of his mind
with rage, and king, he could hardly blame
himself, so he looked to Phoenician cowards
and traitors and cut off several heads.
This display of his imperial pique
did not sit well with Persia's allies.
The Phoenicians he hadn't killed retired
and sailed for home with Egypt's fleet
hard in their wake. Alone now, Xerxes,   390
retreated to Sardis to sulk and to realize
the war was essentially over. If Athens
prefers to think it won its triumph
by its own gallant efforts, the playwright
will not begrudge them a prettier story.
A little embellishment? What's the harm?
The Persians, either way, are losers.
The Greeks, by their valor or merely luck,
have won. As their prize, they get to pick
or even invent what version they like.   400

QUEEN

Wave on wave, a sea of troubles,
breaks, but tell us how this misfortune
occurred.

HERALD

        Our excellent men, strong,
brave, well-trained and well-equipped,
met their deaths in ugly dishonor,

each one bitter and full of shame.
Consider that one brigade that Xerxes
sent to the island off Salamis,
Psyttaleia, their mission to kill
the shipwrecked Greeks who would swim ashore   410
seeking refuge, as Xerxes assumed.
It wasn't a bad plan, but the Greeks
were waiting for them, a large force
armed to the teeth. Their spears and arrows
darkened the sky; they flung small stones
from slingshots and catapults. Encircled,
there was nothing the Persians could do but stand
and die together, until the Greeks
rushed upon those who were still standing
to end their suffering, hacking, stabbing,   420
dismembering and running through
those few who remained, the unlucky remnant.
Terrible, surely, but making it worse
the rest of us could see them. Xerxes
high on the bluff could watch it happen,
and tears ran down his cheeks and he groaned
in rage and grief, and around him, his captains,
seeing and hearing their emperor's cries,
felt beneath their glittering breastplates
the leaden knowledge that all was lost.   430

PROLOGUE

Isn't it lovely? Shall we hear it
one more time? We can, if we like.
This is a play.

HERALD

Our excellent men,
strong, brave, well trained and equipped,
met their deaths in ugly dishonor,
each one bitter and full of shame.

Consider that one brigade that Xerxes
sent to the island off Salamis,
Psyttaleia, their mission to kill
the shipwrecked Greeks who would swim ashore   440
as Xerxes assumed, seeking refuge.
It wasn't a bad plan, but the Greeks
were waiting for them, a large force
armed to the teeth. Their spears and arrows
darkened the sky; they flung small stones
from slingshots and catapults. Encircled
there was nothing the Persians could do but stand
and die together, until the Greeks
rushed upon those who were still standing
to end their suffering, hacking, stabbing,   450
dismembering and running through
those few who remained, the unlucky remnant.
Terrible, surely, but making it worse
the rest of us could see them. Xerxes
high on the bluff could watch as it happened,
and tears ran down his cheeks and he groaned
in rage and grief, and around him, his captains,
seeing and hearing their emperor's cries,
felt beneath their glittering breastplates
the leaden knowledge that all was lost.   460

QUEEN

He thought . . . But how do I, his mother,
know what he thought? I believed, somehow,
that after Marathon heaven owed us . . .
Retribution? Recompense?
He thought to punish the men of Athens
for the Persian grief at Marathon.
Instead, he opened the old wound
and we bled afresh. But tell me, herald,
what ships escaped? Where are they now?
What happened afterward?

HERALD

O queen,   470
Those captains who could fled in disorder
running before the wind. The army
Xerxes commanded headed north
to fight and die on the plain of Euboea
or dwindle from hunger, thirst, disease,
and exhaustion, and then to die a death
few soldiers even imagine.
To come to the point, madame, the army
mostly drowned, in Macedon,
where an early freeze had covered a river   480
with ice on which we thought we could cross.
The first who went at dawn had no
trouble, but then, as the sun beat down
as if to spite us, the ice rotted.
Platoons, brigades sank together
and drowned as each one tried to climb
his companion's back.

And those who died there
were lucky, I think. The rest marched on,
hungry, thirsty, whipped, ashamed,
and heading home to days of dishonor   490
and nights of horrible dreams from which
they will wake to remember worse nightmares,
unbearable memories, terrible things
I have not had the heart to tell you,
that define their lives and histories.

FIRST CHORISTER

How dismaying! Why did the gods
raise our hopes only to dash them?

SECOND CHORISTER

How can we bear such news? How can we
go on living when all our meaning
and purpose is lost? What do we do?   500

PROLOGUE

O Khshayarsha! (That's his name
in Persian.) Son of Daryavaush!
(In Greek, they are Xerxes and Darius!)
This is not merely what some playwright
dreamed up for actors to say on a stage.
The gods wrote this, those astonishing stylists,
masters of every elegant trope.
Atheists out there, agnostics, Quakers,
Unitarians, Christians, and Jews,
each of you in your joys and sorrows   510
calls on the fates, and blesses or curses
or merely inquires how it can be
that a life's random events become
a story, instructive and frequently painful.
Believe! It happens still, today,
as the gods decree—as it happened to them.

QUEEN

Terrible, terrible. But I knew . . .
My dreams had told me. My heart had warned
what you, my counselors, could not see
or would not tell me. What's to be done?   520
I shall offer prayers to Earth and the gifts
of seed cakes to the dead we mourn
and I shall ask for some kind of future
we can bear. Among yourselves
consider what can be done for those few
who do return. If my son appears,
offer him comfort. Escort him home
with his burden of woes I dread to hear.
(Exit Queen.)

CHORUS

I grieve for the Persian men,
but also their mothers and wives,   530
in Agbatana and Susa.
What will they do with their lives?

FIRST CHORISTER

> The women of Persia will weep,
> clutching in empty beds
> those pillows on which their husbands
> used to lay their heads.

SECOND CHORISTER

> They will drench their chadours with tears
> and under their veils will rake
> their ashen cheeks with their sharp
> nails. And our hearts will break.   540

THIRD CHORISTER

> Their voluptuous youth is lost,
> wasted. The wine has turned
> to vinegar now in our goblets,
> and the roasted meats are burned.

FIRST CHORISTER

> Asia herself is bereaved
> and her time of glory ended.
> Europe now has surpassed us,
> powerful, proud, and splendid.

SECOND CHORISTER

> We watched as they marched to war,
> impressive, their armor gleaming   550
> bright. And we shake our heads
> in fear that we are not dreaming.

CHORUS

> Oh, moan, moan in anguish.
> Men live and men must die,
> but the death of a people, a nation . . . How
> do we go on living? We hear the cry
> of drowning men that the seabirds echo,
> and feel the cold of the fishes' kiss.

This is what Persia's ambition has come to.
How do we learn to live with this?   560

SECOND CHORISTER
The Greeks will come to our city,
wanting to settle scores.
They will enslave our children
and use our daughters as whores.

THIRD CHORISTER
The nations of Asia feared us.
That fear restrained their hate
they have been waiting for such
a chance to demonstrate.

FIRST CHORISTER
We'll learn to welcome their insults
as punishments for our crime   570
of merely having survived
to this ignominious time.

THIRD CHORISTER
Those dead men whom we pity,
we'll envy, for they are excused
from seeing their parents and children
demeaned, defiled, and abused.

SECOND CHORISTER
For all we know, this defeat
is a judgment the gods have sent
to show us how those we ruled
suffered and make us repent.   580

PROLOGUE
Where can he go now? Are there limits
to the celebration of Schadenfreude?
Even Aeschylus' fans admit

that his is a somewhat dour view.
But this is a play. We want
some twist, some revelation, some—
dare I say it?—entertainment!
(Enter Queen.)

QUEEN

My good friends, to good times
we became accustomed. That was the world,
or so we thought. Now when evil   590
befalls us shall we repeat that same
mistake and assume that only worse
can follow? My eyes have seen much,
but let me never suppose I know
what is about to happen. This
only the gods and the quiet dead
can tell us. Therefore, I have come
from the palace, alone, to make libation
of milk and honey and water and wine
and the sweet oil of the olive to Earth   600
from which we came, and to which one day
we shall all return. Let us pray to the dead
for knowledge, or patience, or resignation,
or whatever it is within their gift
that can help us know. I call on Darius
and pay to his ghost the reverence and honor
due to the greatest of nether gods.

FIRST CHORISTER

O Queen, we join you in your prayers.
But what can we pray for? How can Darius
lighten the burden we bear?

SECOND CHORISTER

                              O Queen,   610
pour your libations! Let him come.

Darius, during his life, protected
and loved his people. Let him appear
and show us a remedy.

THIRD CHORISTER

                    O Queen,
To go down to death's dominion is easy,
but then to return . . . That's quite a different
matter, for even a great king
may not be able to rise again.
We ask, but we must prepare ourselves
for disappointment. This grief, perhaps,   620
we may be forced to endure alone.

CHORUS

O master of masters, appear,
from the underworld, gloomy and black,
return. Your children invoke you here
in grief. O King Darius, come back!
(*The Ghost of Darius rises and appears.*)

DARIUS

What do you want? What is this?
My wife is standing here at my tomb looking like shit!
And you all have long faces? What's the trouble?

FIRST CHORISTER

We are ashamed to say, your highness.

DARIUS

Are you mad? You call me up this way,   630
and you are ashamed to tell me why?
A thousand heads I took, and yours I left.

SECOND CHORISTER

It is too horrible to say, too vile . . .

DARIUS

What foolishness! You're building up suspense?
You're making for a nice dramatic moment?
This isn't eternity you know, but the real world.
Spit it out! Tell me what horrible, vile,
or shameful thing has happened.
(to the Queen)
You tell me, then. Quickly, directly.
Simply. Now!

QUEEN

          I envy you   640
your death before this dreadful news.

DARIUS

What? What news?

QUEEN

          Persia is destroyed.

DARIUS

How? A famine? Civil war? An earthquake?
What happened?

QUEEN

          The Greeks have destroyed our navy
and beaten our army.

DARIUS

Who was leading? How did he manage to lose
both on land and at sea?

QUEEN

Xerxes, your son.

DARIUS
    He crossed the Bosporus? How?

QUEEN
    He constructed a bridge. He led his army across . . .   650

DARIUS
    A land war in Europe? A monstrous
    perversion of what the fates had ordained.
    An act of ignorant hubris! One who is set
    on ruin may always look to the gods
    for help. Had the boy gone utterly mad?

QUEEN
    Wicked counselors advised him. They looked
    to the wealth your arms had won and wanted
    more, to extend, to complete your work
    of uniting the whole world.

DARIUS
                    I see.
    It never crossed anyone's mind to be grateful   660
    for what we had? On the throne of Persia
    kings of kings presided over
    a mighty empire Medus and Cyrus
    built and I extended . . . But Asian
    and African! The Europeans
    are different from us. And overweening
    pride on Xerxes' part has brought us
    only woe, for which there is no
    cure or even mitigation.

FIRST CHORISTER
    This is sound advice, I am sure,   670
    but it comes too late to be of use.

DARIUS

    Too late for you, perhaps. But him?
    Over there? Look at his smug grin.
    He's enjoying every moment.
(He walks out of the scene and over the the lectern at the proscenium
                 where the Prologue is standing.)
    You, yes, I'm talking to you.
    This is what you want to hear, is it not?

PROLOGUE *(pointing out to the auditorium)*
    What they want, or some of them do.
    I'm here as a kind of referee.
    I try as well as I can to be fair
    to all sides.

DARIUS

            I have no doubt.   680
    Not a patriotic bone in your body,
    I'm sure, as you'll swear by all the gods
    you don't believe in. Neither do they.
    But take it from me, the gods exist,
    and they raise the nations up and dash them
    down again, as you have all seen.
    That more or less fictitious fellow
    from Athens, of whom you've spoken sometimes,
    can also learn that the overweening
    pride of Xerxes is not a peculiarly   690
    Persian failing. Alexander
    will come along in a matter of moments
    and accomplish what Xerxes tried to do.
    And it won't make any difference whatever,
    or not so you'd notice, for Romans will come,
    and Visigoths and Huns . . . The crop
    is corpses, and widows and orphans will offer
    sacrificial cakes of clotted gore
    salted with tears. Your Athenian dandy

who comes to the theater now and again   700
for the poetry but also to gloat,
will go to hell—or whatever he calls it—
and he will see what I have seen.
(He turns and addresses the audience directly.)
You out there! You are proud of this century?
You think you're smarter than we were? Better?
More enlightened? Slavery, torture,
and genocide are your spectator sports.
It's a wonder you still bother with the Theater.
Life outside is ghastly enough, I should think
to suit the most jaded taste, and free every night   710
on the evening news. Go ahead! Gloat—if you dare!
(He glares at the audience, glares for an instant at Prologue, then returns
to the scene.)

SECOND CHORISTER
You haven't left us? You're still here?

DARIUS
Still here. To tell you what you know
already—that men are not to be trusted.
Their plans, lacking in wisdom, always go wrong.
Better than any wisdom is modest prudence,
and faith in the gods, from whom our rewards must come
and punishments too. Accept them, either way.
The Persian army venturing into Greece
destroyed their temples, polluted their altars. The statues   720
of gods were knocked down from their bases. This violation
of measure and manners and order is more than enough
to bring any empire down, as the Greeks will learn
in a short while. And others who follow. We prospered
and could not enjoy our prosperity, were not content
with the rich lot we'd been given. The gods are correct
to chastise such greedy and petulant children. Susa,
is sad, but from this lesson who will learn

in Athens, Rome, Paris, Berlin, Moscow,
Belfast, Dubrovnik, Sarajevo . . . ?   730
(He sighs and gives it up as hopeless. Then he speaks to the Queen.)
You are his mother, madame. Go to the palace
and put on your richest robes to welcome your son
in honor, for he will come in grief, his garments
torn in mourning for what he has lost,
lives, goods and hopes. Now, I go back
to the darkness from which I came.
(He is about to leave, but he has another thought.)
                                    I leave you only
one word of advice—look to the small pleasures
along the way. Nothing else lasts or matters.
Ambition, power, wealth, and all the rest,
none of us misses down there. But a cold drink   740
on a hot day? What more can one want?
(Ghost of Darius descends.)

FIRST CHORISTER
        The pain we feel as acute is also
        chronic—but how can we inure
        ourselves to all feeling? Our only
        comfort is ignorance—which seems to continue
        no matter how vivid or frequent the lessons.

QUEEN
        My heart was broken before, but now
        my soul is shattered. And worse is yet
        to come—my son, whom I love as myself
        is about to appear in even greater   750
        pain that I shall also feel,
        as a mother must, along with my own.
        Offering comfort as well as I can,
        I may not let him see me grieving,

lest I add to his troubled spirit's
burden another leaden weight.
(Exit Queen.)

FIRST CHORISTER
When life was good, comfortable, ordered,
how could we not understand and enjoy
our good fortune? A powerful king,
but fair and even merciful, reigned.   760
Who arose from his bed each morning
to offer prayers of thanks for peace,
prosperity, and justice?

SECOND CHORISTER
                              Happy
men do not define themselves
as happy, do not understand the risk
they run that at any moment all
they take for granted may disappear.
Your house may burn, your crops may wither,
you livestock may die. From a clear sky
killing hail or violent tornadoes   770
may set upon you. But who will fear,
when the sun is shining, the storms of life?
To doubt the kindness of gods and the fates
is perhaps to give offense. They may
on that account withdraw their blessings.

THIRD CHORISTER
Only now, in rueful hindsight
can we understand those pleasant days.
We swam like fish in a shining sea
of miracles and could not imagine
anything else.

FIRST CHORISTER

           Our empire stretched   780
across the sea, from the off-shore islands
of Samos, Chios, and Lesbos beyond
to Lemnos, Rhodes, Knidos, and Cyprus.
Wealth from our tributaries flowed
to make our city splendid, and we
took no joy of it. Malcontents,
we looked for more, were lazy, greedy,
vain, and stupid, all of us!

PROLOGUE

                   Exactly!
Exactly so. What Darius' ghost
said here just now is true, I'm afraid,   790
but that doesn't undo this war,
or Persia's defeat and humiliation,
this bringing down of vanity. Asia's
moment is over. The world is now
Greek, or anyway European.
Asians and Africans may well object,
resenting our culture's success. I say
let them complain. Enjoy their complaining!
Take it as grudging reliable praise
for what we have done and will do and are.   800
(He thinks for a moment and then resumes in a new tone.)
But enough of this horsing around. The time
has come for Xerxes to make his entrance.
What we are about to see is no
joke, for if this is a tragedy, Xerxes
must be its hero. We only have
a couple of hundred lines that remain
in Aeschylus' text. Let's give him a hearing
and see what the ruined King of Persia
can say for himself.
                  You know, in Greek,

they give important proper nouns 810
an article—as we do to "The Bronx."
They would say, "The New York," "The Boston,"
"The Washington" but . . . "Baltimore."
In just that way, they gave their little
honorific to kings—except
for the ruler of Persia.
　　　　　　　　And here he comes.
(Enter Xerxes alone.)

XERXES
　　I hate this. Among the many
　　terrible moments, this is . . . another.
　　To see them standing there, the old
　　subjects and citizens . . . The gods 820
　　who abandoned me are not required
　　to endure these baleful and accusing
　　looks or hear their just complaints—
　　for they believed in me, revered
　　and trusted in what I thought and did.
　　But I have betrayed them.
　　　　　　　　O gods!
　　I should have died on the battlefield,
　　my corpse another among the heap
　　that lay on the beach or one that floated,
　　ghastly and pale in the greenish water. 830

FIRST CHORISTER
　　Alas for the mighty king who returns
　　thus. Alas for Xerxes!

SECOND CHORISTER
　　　　　　　　Alas
　　for the dead, the myriad dead, the archers,
　　the spearmen, the sailors, the Persian heroes.

XERXES

Alas for the woe I bring to my people.
Alas for my people, who hate me.

FIRST CHORISTER

                                        Alas
for the hatred, the grief, the contempt.

THIRD CHORISTER

Weep and wail. Give voice to anger!
Persia cries. Persia cries out.

XERXES

A vile change! A terrible thing!   840
The wounded called out in pain, and the dead
moan in their endless imprecations
the living echo. Alas for Persia!

FIRST CHORISTER

Where are the others? Where are your noble
fighters? Pharandakas? Sousas?
Pelagon and Agabatas?
Dotammas, Psammis, Sousiscanes?

XERXES

Dead. Every one of them dead,
their bodies pulp for the sea-birds' lunch.

SECOND CHORISTER

Oh alas, and where is Pharnouchus?   850
And Ariomardus, and Seualkes?
Lilaeus, Memphis, Tharybdis.
These were my friends. Where are they now?

XERXES

What can I tell you? Dead. Gone.
Lost at sea, or hacked to pieces,

or drowned under the river ice . . .
The flower of Persia, these noble men . . .
It breaks my heart to hear their names.

THIRD CHORISTER

How could you do such a thing? How can you
stand there and tell us . . . Sesames too?   860
And Batanochus' brave son Alpistus?
Parthus, and Oebares? You left them
behind? How could you?

XERXES

                    Oh, alas.
What would you have me say? How can I
express my regret, and shame, and grief?

FIRST CHORISTER

We have our own griefs. We need
no instructions of yours to feel
pain without limit. We mourn for Xanthes,
the leader of ten thousand fighters,
and Angchares and Diaexis   870
and Arsamas, the masters of horsemen,
and Dadakas, Lythimnas, and Tolmus
whose spear was drenched with enemy blood . . .
Where are they? Your retinue,
your imperial guard? Your mighty host?
We look around and no one is there
but you. The vista is empty.

XERXES

                    I know.
I know, I know. Oh, woe!
Gone, every one. All those names . . .
not even marked on a foreign gravestone.   880

SECOND CHORISTER
You have done this! You have brought
disaster upon us. Grief beyond
all possible measure.

THIRD CHORISTER
                    You!
You, you son of a bitch! You!

XERXES
Go ahead, rant. Nothing you say
can even come near what I think, myself.

FIRST CHORISTER
Does that give us any consolation?

XERXES
You see what my kingdom has come to.

THIRD CHORISTER
                              We see!
Nothing! You are the king of nothing.

FIRST CHORISTER
We were the lords of the world, and now   890
we are slaves! And butts of Greek jokes.

SECOND CHORISTER
So many went. So few returned.

THIRD CHORISTER
You are the curse of the Persians.

XERXES
                    I know!
You see, I have torn my royal garments.

SECOND CHORISTER
    What good does that do us?

THIRD CHORISTER
                    What good
does it do the dead, or their widows and orphans?

XERXES
    Your harsh words do not offend me,
    but resonate in my soul. We sing
    our songs of woe in harmonious chorus,
    antiphonal anthems of utter chagrin.   900

FIRST CHORISTER
    That's too easy. You cannot hate
    yourself with the hatred the rest of us feel!

XERXES
    How do you know? I can! I do!

SECOND CHORISTER
    If you did, you wouldn't be standing there.
    You'd have taken poison or cut your wrists,
    or fallen on your sword.

XERXES
              Not so!
    I thought of that, of course. But death
    would have been an easy end to my pain.
    To continue to live was worse. To return
    to hear your complaints, to endure your rage,   910
    and to punish myself as I witness your grief.

THIRD CHORISTER
    Not enough. There isn't a torment
    in all the world that even comes close.

You absurd son-of-a-bitch, you impossible
shit! You perverse fuck! Fuck you!
(Prologue raises his hands to stop the action, but this time to no effect.
This time, Xerxes and the chorus take no notice
of him.)

SECOND CHORISTER
You could blind yourself, as Oedipus did.

XERXES
I thought of that, but to see your faces,
to read your expressions of woe and contempt
seemed even worse than continual darkness.

SECOND CHORISTER
There must be something you can do.   920
Just to continue to live and breathe
and see and hear and feel is not
enough.

THIRD CHORISTER
But nothing's enough. Our hatred
knows no limits. You motherfucker!
Ass-hole! Scumbag.

PROLOGUE
Gentlemen, please . . .
Let us maintain . . .

THIRD CHORISTER *(interrupting)*
Who the hell are you?
What business of yours is this? Fuck off!

PROLOGUE
This is a play. I am the prologue . . .

XERXES
>Oh, god! A play?

THIRD CHORISTER
>>It's no fucking play!
>The battle was real. Those dead soldiers
>are real. Persia is real, you dickhead!

930

PROLOGUE
>It's still a play.

FIRST CHORISTER *(mournfully)*
>>It doesn't matter.

PROLOGUE
>But it does. Out there, an Athenian watches,
>or a whole roomful of Greeks. Your griefs
>will be on display forever.

XERXES
>>Oh, god!
>He's right, of course. My torments will stretch
>endlessly into the future. And yours,
>your hatred, your feeling of having been
>betrayed, and your grief will hang in the air
>like bad smells that won't go away.

940

THIRD CHORISTER
>Cat piss is like that! You know, Xerxes?
>Cat piss is what you have made of us all!

PROLOGUE
>I am afraid we've gone as far as we can.
>There's nothing left to say. The play
>may as well end here.

SECOND CHORISTER

                    Up your ass!
We don't take orders from you.

XERXES

                    He's right.

PROLOGUE
Never mind me. It's them, out there.
They have to go to work in the morning.
They have trains to catch. They've seen
enough, I should think . . .

XERXES

                         There's never enough!   950
The rage of the chorus is in their hearts.
The contempt of Greeks for Persians, they share
in their bigoted hearts. And the craving I had
for glory and conquest is theirs as well.
If they were kings, they'd do exactly
as I have done. It's the way men are,
and women too, I might add.

FIRST CHORISTER

                    No, sir,
you are not a hero. There is no
hero here. You cannot have
the last word.

SECOND CHORISTER

          And what is that?   960

THIRD CHORISTER
Something nasty . . . an odor of cat piss.
(Xerxes covers his head with his cloak. Blackout.)

Seven Against Thebes

Translated by
Stephen Sandy

Translator's Preface

What you get is not what you see in the text of *Seven Against Thebes*. The play is an apex, the climactic third of a trilogy we lack. From a great corpus of Aeschylean plays, only one trilogy survives complete, the *Oresteia*. Presumptively the trilogy from which the *Seven* comes was similar in structure to the *Oresteia*. But the plays that lead up to the *Seven* went missing in antiquity, and all we have are scattered hints. Until the mid-nineteenth century the play was thought to be the second in a lost trilogy. But a scrap of papyrus surfaced that revealed the names of the preceding plays, *Laius* and *Oedipus*, and showed us that *Seven* came last—yet nothing more, other than the date of its production (467 B.C.) and the fact that it won first prize.[1]

We must not attempt to see the plays of this Theban trilogy through the grid of the *Oresteia*. For there is a more primordial aspect to *Seven*.[2] As in a palimpsest, primitive concerns and motives show through. This play finds its roots in tales of pollution, violence, and oracular (Delphic) cult worship. In the war at the gates of Thebes between Theban defenders and Argive challengers, one critic even finds a conflict between the supporters of an Olympian orthodoxy—the new hegemonic order in Aeschylus' world, represented by the Thebans—and the Argives, figures of an earlier (and outmoded) order of shamanist practices, chiefly signaled by the type of mantic seer, Amphiaraus.

Amphiaraus reluctantly joined the Argives against Thebes; as a shaman he knew he would die. Thus among the seven challengers his shield alone is emblazoned with no device; this blank, this imageless message forbodes the doom of the attackers. At the Cadmean walls he cries to Tydeus:

1. D. J. Conacher, *Aeschylus: The Earlier Plays and Related Studies* (Toronto: University of Toronto Press, 1996), pp. 36ff.

2. Jack Lindsay, *The Clashing Rocks: A Study of Early Greek Religion and Culture and the Origins of Drama* (London: Chapman and Hall, 1965), pp. 48, 154–70.

" . . . I'll fertilize your soil with this,
my flesh, a seer interred in a foreign land . . ."
So spoke the prophet, serene, and raised his shield.
No heraldry emblazoned it, for he would not
appear, but *be*: intending excellence
not pretense, while he gathered from the folds
of his mind the fruits from which his wisdom came.
(640–41, 643–47)

Moreover, in such a probing reading there is evidence of a "weapons cult" in the extraordinary attention paid to warmaking gear, in particular the shields and their devices, making the war into a duel of images on shields and the opposing sides' opposed interpretations of their meanings.

The titles of the plays preceding *Seven* make clear, in broad outline, what went before. Recall the story of Laius and Oedipus. Laius married Jocasta of the royal family of Thebes; together they ruled over Thebes but remained childless. When Laius consulted the Oracle at Delphi he was told to be grateful for childlessness since any child would be his murderer; Laius having inadvertently slept with Jocasta, a son was born. In the usual version of the story, Laius, to save himself, took the infant, pierced his feet with a spike, and exposed him on a mountainside. A shepherd found the child, however, named him Oedipus ("swellfoot," for the handicap of his wounded feet), and took him to Corinth, where he was raised by the Corinthian king, Polybus, and his queen. As a youth, Oedipus went to the Delphic Oracle to learn his future and was told that he would kill his father and marry his mother; whereupon, loving his adoptive family, he fled Corinth to put himself and his presumed parents out of harm's way.

Soon Laius himself set out for Delphi to ask the Oracle how to rid Thebes of the Sphinx, a monster that had jinxed his city (at Hera's behest) and was devouring each person who could not answer a riddle the Sphinx posed. Laius met Oedipus on a narrow road, telling him to stand aside and let his chariot pass. Oedipus refusing to do so, Laius sideswiped the young stranger and ran over his foot. Infuriated, Oedipus killed Laius. Oedipus proceeded to Thebes, guessed the riddle of the Sphinx, and thus rid the city of its bane.

The Thebans in gratitude made him their king, he married his mother

Jocasta, and they had children: Polynices and Eteocles, who for Oedipus were sons and brothers; Ismene and Antigone, sisters as well as daughters. When Oedipus learned of his crime, he blinded himself and departed to spend the rest of his life wandering in penance and exile. But not before cursing his sons, who he foretold would die, each by the hand of the other.

These events must have been the substance of the two plays preceding our play, though what treatment Aeschylus gave them and what dramaturgy he employed to present his use of the myth, no one knows. Nevertheless, the stories set the stage for the drama of *Seven Against Thebes*. The Thebans—or Creon, brother of the now-dead Jocasta—elect Eteocles and Polynices rulers of Thebes. They are to rule alternately, year by year. Eteocles, however, refuses to give up his power, and Polynices with help of his father-in-law Adrastus and others returns to force Eteocles to give him his due.

The relation between the two brothers, said to be twins, needs another word of explanation. Recorders of myth suggest several answers as to why Oedipus curses his sons. Oedipus might be expressing feelings of guilt and horror at his relationship to these princes, whom he has fathered yet who are his brothers. It is also held that the curse comes when one of the sons gives Oedipus wine in a cup that had belonged to Laius—recalling for Oedipus his initial crime—and the other gives him an inferior cut of meat from a sacrificial animal. This lack of proper form at mealtime has the ring of truth as the cause for the paternal curse, appropriate to the hieratic vendettas of ancient Greek family strife. Oedipus received the haunch, according to Robert Graves, rather than the royal shoulder, an act that would have "amounted to a denial of divine authority."[3] But all these matters have been dealt with, these questions posed—and answered—before this play begins. The Eteocles of Aeschylus is no deceitful, power-mad brother, jealous of Polynices' rightful place; rather he is portrayed throughout as the virtuous and commendable commander of Thebes, giving himself wholly to the preservation of the *polis* he guards.

"Works of art are of an infinite loneliness," Rilke wrote in *Letters to a Young Poet*, "and with nothing so little to be reached as with criticism." The

3. Robert Graves, *The Greek Myths* (Baltimore: Penguin Books, 1959), 2: 14.

Seven will always have its loneliness, its mystery, and yet we must come to terms with it as best we can. Not long ago, when I had only recently finished making the version of the play that follows, I attended a performance by Kadmus Theatre Studio of *Cinders of Thebes*, a play taken from *Seven*. It moved me, stuck in my mind, clung to my dreams. *Cinders of Thebes*, directed by Bill Reichblum, acknowledged and celebrated Aeschylus' sacred intent, his hieratic stylization and emphasis on ritual (as in the matter of the shields). Reichblum let this formal power inspire a version—a rendition— of scenes from *Seven* in which dance, song, and difficult movement requiring strength and gymnastic agility largely supplanted the speeches of the text. The dramaturgy did not so much describe the sacral rages of the Aeschylean tragedy as embody them.

What had long troubled me in the *Seven* was its static quality; there was so much danger and rage, yet most of the play was taken up by the choosing of the champions to defend the city as a result of the scout's lengthy descriptions of the challengers and their shields. But here was the point. The device on each shield must be interpreted—first the Argive viewpoint, then the Theban. Which is the true meaning? It is all a matter of hermeneutics. The severe power of language, the power of an image—whether visual or articulated in language—is central to the meaning of the play; once a shield is seen, its device described in words, the challenger is known, the power of his image has been met—if not canceled. When the final challenger is announced—Polynices, brother of Eteocles—there is no choice for Eteocles but to take up the challenge, a duel fated to be the prophesied fraternal Armageddon, and fulfill the words of the curse placed on the brothers by their father.

The isolation of this tragedy has long made it obscure, its stylized grandeur not only mysterious and sacred but also suggestive of a sublime context (which it may not deserve—and might lack if we knew just what treatment of its themes in the *Laius* and the *Oedipus* it caps. "Nothing lost, nothing sacred"). *Seven Against Thebes* must have originally been called by another name, for this title does not describe the completing arc of action in the tragedy (and Aeschylus himself never mentions "Thebes" in the play; it is always the Cadmean city or the bastion of Cadmus). As we have seen, the play was thought to be the central member of a lost trilogy until it was found to have been the final play in that trilogy. Consequently it was realized that the conclusion of the play, its third movement if you will, represents interpolation, or substitution for a lost closure; at any rate a corruption of the Aeschylean original. No mention of Antigone or Ismene is made until they enter; indeed, anterior passages affirm that with the death of Polynices and Eteocles the line of Laius will be totally extinct. Thus not only the intrusion of the sisters, but also the shift in tone and pace, suggest an ancient, substantive emendation. For detailed argument we must turn to the scholars. In the face of baffling choices and certain uncertainty, we must make our own surmise—and the best of what comes down to us.

The painter Rubens remarked, in a letter to Franciscus Junius in 1637, that the works of the ancients are seen "only in the imagination, like dreams, or so obscured by words, that we try in vain to grasp them (as Orpheus the shade of Eurydice)."[4] In 1996, Robert Potter noted that "we are, in fact, living in a great age of stage translation and adaptation. . . . This is precisely because contemporary poets have taken this creative responsibility into their own hands . . . there are many different paths to a successful transmission of a play from one linguistic community to another."[5]

This is a poet's version of a remote and haunting text, whose august stance is hard to comprehend, let alone take great delight in or terror from. When I saw the Kadmus Theatre production of matter from this play, I knew that the delicately brutal singing and dancing had unpacked that mystery for me. The translation (there by Peter Arnott) paled before the intensity of the moment; Reichblum's conception dealt out in swaggering song and prancing dance around the circle of the stage I and the rest of the audience sat crosslegged to mark. For the strange life and sacral texture of *Seven Against Thebes* seem so distant as to defy us, as if the words themselves wore masks. And this, remember, is a drama to be performed before a huge audience in the theater of Dionysus, with judges in their marble thrones along the first row, not a text to be assayed in pondering and ponderous essays considering the flotsam of its links to other tragedies or scribal drift in the transmission.

My aim has not been, nor could have been, to make a scholarly and exact

---

4. " . . . quae sola imaginatione tanquam somnia se nobis offerunt et verbis tantum adumbrata ter frustra comprensa (ut Orpheum Euridices imago) . . . " With thanks to Julius S. Held for calling attention to Rubens' remark. Held, "Carolus Scribanius's Observations on Art in Antwerp," *Journal of the Warburg and Courtauld Institutes* 59 (1996): 174–204.

5. Robert Potter. Communication to the *Times Literary Supplement*, November 1996.

rendering (for this, many texts are at hand), but to find a voice and tempo that would give the effect of the play's sacerdotal solemnity and stately ceremony; and to offer a style that might be formal yet not call attention to itself—as with the bright bosses of rhyme. (Rhymed couplets worked with wonderful effect in the lighter and more familiar world of Euripides' *Helen* as translated by Rachel Hadas. The relaxed and pleasing elegance of Hadas' verse made a recent New York production scintillate.) As Kazuo Okakura, quoting a Ming scholar, reminds us, translation is possible but is like the back side of a brocade: the threads are there, but the colors, the design, is not, or only faintly so; it's there, but reversed. So it must be with this version.

The faults in the pages that follow are my own. I have received salutary encouragement from David Slavitt. My chief debt must be to Malcolm D. Hyman, who has cheerfully given valuable advice and correction at every point. Without his informed and generous assistance this work could not have been completed. My take is apparent in what follows, a rendering of *Seven Against Thebes* that is, I hope, readable and coherent but that is— needless to say—lacking in the artful richness of the original, devoid of the complex grandeur of Aeschylus.

Cast

ETEOCLES, son of Oedipus, king of Thebes
CHORUS of young Theban women
SCOUT
ANTIGONE, sister of Eteocles
ISMENE, sister of Eteocles
HERALD
NONSPEAKING
   Melanippus
   Polyphontes
   Megareus
   Hyperbius
   Actor
   Lasthenes

*(Eteocles, ruler of Thebes, downstage, addresses the audience. He is
alone as his harangue begins, but soon, very slowly, first one then
another member of the chorus of six young women appears from
the wings, tentatively at first, then moving distractedly behind
Eteocles in a pantomime of anguish.)*

ETEOCLES
   Men of the city of Cadmus:
Your commander-in-chief, on twenty-four-hour watch,
who guards your welfare from the bridge of state
and mans the helm, must speak to the issue at hand.
Success in this great engagement will be due
to a god: but any failure will be ours.
I will be blamed, my name shouted, echoing
in Theban streets with the people's cries and groans.
May Zeus the protector guard the Cadmeans' city
and ward us from this fate.   10

Now every one of you, those under age
and those too old to be called up but fit,
as well as each man of age to join this draft,
must enlist to serve the state, its altars, and its gods.
Its honorable estate must not be stained
or perish from the earth. You must do it for your children;
and as much, or more, for Earth, your nurse and mother,
who took your pains as hers; for, when you crawled
on her breast or were a wavering toddler, she raised you
with love to bear reliable shields for her   20
in this, her day of crisis.
                         So far, the gods
are with us; long we've held our walls, but the battle—
gods willing it so—has gone our way. Seize
the hour, now that our master augur, knowing
and feeling along his veins and nerves, detects—
infallibly divines!—this very night
the major Argive force decides to move
against us.
(Enter two choristers stage left.)
                         Every man in battle gear!
Man your battle stations—climb the walls, the towers;
watch every access. Meet them at the gates   30
in fighting trim: give no thought to numbers,
how many the enemy may be! For the gods
decide the day.
                         On my part I have sent out
reconnaissance teams, pickets to help me make
decisions; and warn of ambush well in advance.
(Enter Scout stage right.)

SCOUT
     Cadmean lord!
                    Respectfully, sir, I bring
intelligence; reliable reports of enemy forces

at the walls. With my own eyes I have seen them!
seven volunteers—all aces, picked or chosen
I cannot tell, but officers who've taken vows—   40
butchered a bull, and in the hollow of a shield
gathered dark blood; handled steaming gore—
and sworn by Ares and Terror, who lust for blood,
to level Thebes—or, falling, turn our soil
to bloody mire. Then they pinned mementos
to the chariot of Adrastus, homeward bound,
tokens of themselves for parents, at which tears fell—
but no complaint. Courage had steeled their hearts
raised to a pitch by valor.
(Two more choristers enter upstage.)
                              They stood possessed
as lions on the prowl, warlike, glaring in a field.   50
My report here is not a sluggard's: I got away
just as it was decided who, by luck of the draw,
would march against which gate. Therefore, dispatch
our best troops now, for now the Achaeans, armed
from head to foot, raise dust toward every gate;
froth from the horses' throats sprays the field
out there—scatters like sea-foam in onshore wind.
Now then, our pilot, our captain, secure the bulkheads
of our vessel, our city, before the storm strikes,
for the wave of their invasion crashes against   60
the dry shore of Thebes! Do these things now,
while I remain true sentinel—night and day
ever on faithful watch—and you, receiving
my clear intelligence, shall stand unscathed.
(Exit Scout.)

ETEOCLES
        O Zeus and Earth, and deities that guard the city,
        and evil curse—powerful instrument
        of my begetter's rage—I pray: do not

annihilate our city, for our tongue is Greek;
or raze our homes to hearth- and threshold-stones.
(Other chorus members enter stage left and right.)
May the Achaeans never reduce the free   70
city of Cadmus to bonds of slavery. Guard us!
We have a common purpose here, I know;
states that survive give honors to their gods.
(Exit Eteocles. Last members of chorus enter; they move as in a dance
and speak severally at first.)

CHORUS LEADER
We cry aloud for fear,
the armies leave their camps.

SECOND CHORISTER
Woe, they are coming here,

THIRD CHORISTER
like a mounting tide they move
upon our shore,

FOURTH CHORISTER
the first
wave must be horse—the dust
from their feet as they tramp   80
spirals into the sky,

FIFTH CHORISTER
silent messenger, but true.

SIXTH CHORISTER
Now the drum of their hooves
on nearer ground reaches
my ear . . . each of us listening,
craning from our corners, fearing

irresistible torrent lashing
the mountainside.

FIRST CHORISTER
                    O gods
and goddesses, turn aside
the swelling horrors! Now
with a shout outside our walls   90
their ranks armed in white
charge up to scale our walls.

SECOND CHORISTER
Now who will save us, what
god or goddess?

THIRD CHORISTER
                    Now where
shall I fall down beseeching,
before the shrines of our
progenitors?

FOURTH CHORISTER
                    I hail
your sacred presences;
high time for us who linger
and lament to cling to these   100
icons of you on earth!

CHORUS LEADER
Will you not hear the clang
of sword on shield?
                    What time
more fit than now to deck
your images with wreath
and robe in supplication?

The sound grows visible; din
and clash of countless spears.

FIFTH CHORISTER

What will you do, Ares,
heir of this soil, forsake   110
this Theban ground, so long
your home? And you, bright god
of the golden helmet, look
on this land you once held dear!

FIRST PAIR OF CHORISTERS

Guardian gods of our city,
all of you, come see this train
of virgin girls praying
to be saved from bondage! Plumes
on helmets flash in the surge
of men, sped by the gale   120
of Ares' breath, that heaves now,
now crashes at our gates.
But Zeus, father of all
good deeds, now turn aside
our capture by this foe.

SECOND PAIR OF CHORISTERS

Circling the fortress of Cadmus, Achaeans now
tighten the noose; with fear we reel as weapons
of war close in, clattering chargers bite,
champing bits chaining their jaws, ringing out
with sound of slaughter. Seven bold captains,   130
socketed spears at the ready: each, unmistakable
among armed men, takes his allotted stand.

THIRD PAIR OF CHORISTERS

Potent with Zeus your parent, Pallas Athena,
avid for battle, save us; prove yourself!
And you, ruler of horses, lord of the abyss

with fish-spearing trident, Poseidon, deliver us
from terror, free us from tyranny of fear.
Ares, O lord of war, you as well, alas
must take pity, come forward as you long have
to care for us, guard the city named for Cadmus.   140
And Cypris, very mother of us all, hear us;
we come to your hallowed altars imploring you:
avert disaster, defend your kin. And you,
Apollo, lord of wolves, impelled by our cries,
bring to our enemy what they would bring, make them
cry out like slaughtering wolves. And you, Artemis,
maiden daughter of Leto, string your bow!

FIRST PAIR OF CHORISTERS

    Aie! I hear the racket of chariots
careening round the walls. Hearken,
O Hera of the skies, the wheels   150
keen under the laden axles' weight!
My beloved Artemis, appear!
What is befalling our city? Hearken,
the air crazes with brandished spears!
What will the gods do with our fear?
How far will they let this peril go?

SECOND PAIR OF CHORISTERS

                      Listen.
Showers of stones from their slingers loft
over the walls into the fortress.
                   Beloved
Apollo! The din of bronze at the gates rises,
sails to our ears on the wind that winces   160
in the tumult of shield clanging on brazen shield.
Victory must go to them with right on their side;
now Zeus must decide the battle. Beloved Athena,
stationed yet in your shrine before our city,
guard your seven-gated seat of honor!

THIRD PAIR OF CHORISTERS
> Gods and goddesses,
> omnipotent to save,
> all you powerful guardians
> of our land and towering Thebes, do not forsake us,
> your city reeling under   170
> onslaught of foreign warriors
> speaking a foreign tongue.
> Hear us, poor girls, with beseeching hands upraised,
> hear us, it is only right; hear our cry.

FIRST PAIR OF CHORISTERS
> Beloved gods who hover
> around the city, keep watch,
> deliver Thebes in this her hardest hour.
> Show how you love us, shield us
> from ruin; we beg you, remember
> our care, our worship, the rites that have abounded   180
> in loving oblations and blood sacrifice.

(Enter Eteocles.)

ETEOCLES
> Hear me, you stupid creatures! Is this the best
> that you can do? Is this the way to save
> the city? Is this the best for hard-pressed troops,
> that you should go salaaming at every shrine?
> Whether it's hard times or good old happy days,
> don't put me with the women! When they're in charge,
> their bossy ways will finish peaceful days,
> and when they scare, they make everything worse
> on the homefront—and for the nation. Just as you,   190
> running around mindlessly up and down,
> make such a hue and cry today as brings on
> panic, mechanical response, instinctive fear,
> by which we aid the enemy and help
> to bring Thebes down!

That's what happens when
a man lives with women. So be it! Anyone
who is not with me all the way—woman
or man or something in between—will get
what he deserves; the crowd will stone him to death.
For action in the field is man's work; don't   200
let women tell us what to do! Let them
weave and breed, doing what they can do,
indoors—and out of our way. You hear? Or am I
preaching to the deaf?

CHORUS *(in unison until after Eteocles exits)*
Noble Eteocles,
Oedipus' son, my spirits
falter hearing the rough
creak and clank of chariots,
of hub on axle sleeve,
the squealing wheels! Listen.   210
Can't you hear it? Like a rudder
in every callused mouth,
the bits of tempered steel
guide each steed, each mouth
jangles as it is steered
in the loud clamor of speed!

ETEOCLES
When the ship in heavy seas is straining, tell me,
does the helmsman desert his post at the stern and rush
fore and aft to save himself from the storm?

CHORUS
Confident always with faith   220
in the gods I hurried to all
these shrines of ancient deities
when from beyond our gates
like a tornado the heavy

shower of missiles rained.
In the hour of fear I drew
nearer my gods with prayer
to save the homeland with their
imperishable power.

ETEOCLES

You pray that our defenses may stand firm   230
against the enemy?

CHORUS

                    They will, with the gods' help.

ETEOCLES

Not so! Conventional wisdom has it that
the gods of a town like ours desert it once
it's captured. The gods don't love you when you're down.

CHORUS

May I never see the enemy
defeat our brave defenders
or plunder these very streets,
torch our buildings, our homes;
never while I live
let those deities yonder   240
falter in standing by me.

ETEOCLES

Don't panic; mix prudence with your piety;
discipline is the mother of success,
the consort of salvation—as they say.

CHORUS

How true that is, and yet
the will of heaven above
is supreme; just when a man
thinks it's the end—heaven

may raise him from despair,
however dark the storm cloud   250
that has dimmed his sight.

ETEOCLES

Just leave it to the men to make due sacrifice
to the gods before the battle. Your duty
is to keep your mouth shut and stay indoors.

CHORUS

It's by the gods' will the city
is not invaded; the ramparts
hold back the tide of foes.
What can be wrong with that?

ETEOCLES

I'm not offended if you honor the gods.
But if you can't keep calm, and yield to terror,   260
you will make cowards of the populace.

CHORUS

When I heard the sudden din,
confusion of weapons clashing,
I flew to the highest ground,
our blessed place of worship.

ETEOCLES

So if you hear of casualties or loss
of life, don't panic at the news and shriek;
for it is with blood the god of war is fed.

CHORUS

But listen! I hear the horses neighing!

ETEOCLES

                                        Then listen,
but not too closely. Keep it to yourself.

CHORUS

The groundworks   270
of the city groan as if foes hemmed us in.

ETEOCLES

I am in charge here. Is not that enough?

CHORUS

The clamor at the gates grows louder. I feel dread.

ETEOCLES

Silence! Say nothing of this abroad in Thebes.

CHORUS

O throng of gods, stand by our battlements now!

ETEOCLES

Keep quiet! Suffer what comes in silence.

CHORUS

Gods of my city, preserve me from slavery!

ETEOCLES

You'll make yourself a slave, and me, and all of us.

CHORUS

Omnipotent Zeus, send lightning bolts against them!

ETEOCLES

Oh, what a sex Zeus made in making women!   280

CHORUS

No worse than men, when Thebes is taken captive.

ETEOCLES

And still you yelp, embracing the gods' images.

CHORUS
   Yes; in my fear, dread commandeers my speech.

ETEOCLES
   Please heaven, you would do me one little favor!

CHORUS
   Ask me right now, I'll tell you if I can.

ETEOCLES
   Hold your tongue, miserable woman, don't panic our men.

CHORUS
   My lips are sealed. I'll meet my doom with the rest.

ETEOCLES
   That's the way to talk, better than before.
   Moreover, I ask you to pray for the best outcome.
   As you leave the penetralium of statues, pray   290
   that the gods may fight on our side. After you
   have heard my own prayers, raise your voices, shout
   in acclamation to heaven our hymn of praise
   sacred to Greek ways, that strengthens friends
   and cancels fear of enemies.
                              And now
   my vow: to all the gods of our country, both
   to those who haunt the countryside and those
   who guard the city square; to Dirce's source
   and to Ismenus' stream, when all is well
   and Thebes is safe again:
                              I vow that we   300
   shall drench your altars with red blood of bulls
   and sheep; and on your walls hang trophies, spears,
   and shirts torn from the foe, spoils of battle
   won in battle, hung up to honor your hallows.
   You women now: add prayers and offerings, not

with sighs or with that sobbing babble as before,
finding that nothing of that sort alters fate.
As for me, I go now to pick six men, and with
myself as seventh, a crew of champions
to man our seven gates and make a stand—   310
quickly now, before bad news brings home
to everyone how desperate the crisis is.
(Exit Eteocles.)

CHORUS LEADER
    I hear what he is saying,
    but my heart is beating fast,
    horror weighs down my spirit,
    it keeps this dread aflame,
    dread for the host that hems
    our walls in—just as a dove,
    a mother trembling as
    she broods over her young,   320
    hovers above the nest
    near the snake that watches.
    Our walls are thick and high,
    but intruders advance, platoons
    in formation closing in,
    tightening the noose. What
    can be done? From every side
    bands of them are slinging
    sharp rocks on the populace.
    What will become of me?   330
    O gods, descended from Zeus, by any means
    preserve our city and men, offspring of Cadmus!

FIRST PAIR OF CHORISTERS
    What better land is there than this, if you
    should abandon us to enemies and have
    to choose another plain to guard? Or water
    finer than flows from Dirce's fountain, stream

unequaled among all those the daughters of Tethys
pour forth, or those that from Poseidon flow?

SECOND PAIR OF CHORISTERS
    Gods of the city, then,
    guarding my ancient town,   340
    now hurl destruction down
    on those outside; send them
    a shock that makes them drop
    their weapons and run for their lives.
    That wins us glory! Amid
    our prayers, that rise from keening,
    defend us; retain the title
    to your city and your thrones!

THIRD PAIR OF CHORISTERS
    To be sure, it would be a pitiful thing to have
    a blackout in a land already gray with age,   350
    the victim of the Argives, captives hauled off
    at spearpoint, a city shamefully done in
    amid the ashes of the Argives' scorched-earth campaign;
    see women young and old alike dragged off
    to bondage by the hair, like horses pulled
    by their manes, their lovely garments stripped away,
    while any untorched precinct of the city fills
    with screams, tumult of getting stripped and trashed,
    the cries of rape, destruction, and despair—
    complete confusion! In dread I see it now,   360
    the weight of this calamity descending.

FIRST PAIR OF CHORISTERS
    Pitiful shame that virgin girls be forced
    before their nubile time and the lawful rites,
    sent horribly from home to alien labors!
    No, I declare the dead are better off than these
    captives who suffer the change of violation.

Oh me, when cities fall, how wretched, how
painful their ordeal, what grief and desolation
find shelter in the ruins of their walls!
One drags another off, or butchers him,   370
then torches the scene, all the whole city soiled
with smoke and the god of war, raving trampler,
mastering the people and fouling, defiling piety.
The streets echo with mayhem; turrets raised
to storm our walls advance and fence us in.
Man cuts down man; the wails of mothers meet
the little cries of nursing infants drenched
in blood. People fleeing take to pillage,
your own kin join in rapine and robbery.
The empty-handed meet and go where looters   380
are bagging booty, each greedy for his share,
and more if possible; plunderer spoiling plunderer.
Can words describe what all of this will mean?

SECOND PAIR OF CHORISTERS
All fruits are plucked or, bruising, fall to earth,
as if a farmer's cart should tip and its produce
roll and scatter in the streets, to the dismay
of the girl in charge. The bounty of the earth, seized
in the commotion by brigands, is swept away
like flotsam adrift on heavy seas. Young girls
as slaves now get their first lesson—to learn   390
the misery of a master's lust; to be
a master's property, as if of a rich husband,
but won at spearpoint. They can only wait
the ruthless spoiler's coming nightly to his bed;
such expectation must be their hope in life.

CHORUS LEADER
Dear girls, I think the scout
brings tidings from the front,
news for our anxious ears;

in haste, as if on wheels,
he sprints.

CHORUS *(in unison)*
         And look, our prince,   400
dear son of Oedipus,
comes—in such a hurry
he nearly stumbles—just
in time to learn the latest.
(Scout and Eteocles—with Melanippus, Polyphontes, Megareus, Hyper-
              bius, Actor, Lasthenes—enter from opposite sides.)

SCOUT
I am reliably informed and will report
the enemy battle plan; how each of their men
proceeded to his post, assigned by lot.
In position for some time at the Proetid gate,
Tydeus hankers for attack but is held back
from crossing the Ismenus by the seer,   410
when sacrificial omens were not auspicious.
So Tydeus, inflamed and spoiling for the fight,
bellows like a bull raging in the noonday heat
and taunts the prophet, Oecles' son; calls him
a coward cringing at the thought of death
and battle. Shouting these words, he shakes his helmet;
it gleams among the shadows of its comb
bobbing with flowing feathers, while beneath
his shield bronze bells menace with a shrill jangle,
and on the shield his proud device, a midnight sky   420
brilliant with stars around a full moon shining,
first among heavenly bodies, the eye of night.
Chafing there by the river bank in a splendor
of armor, the swashbuckling champion roars, obsessed
with combat, like a fierce war-horse that strains
at the bit to hear the trumpet sound the charge.
What combatant will you send to meet him there
and defend the Proetid gate when it is opened?

ETEOCLES

I fear no wounds from signs. Heraldic emblems
won't hurt without a spear. At no man's get-up   430
will I tremble! Indeed, this night you speak of
on his shield may well hold hidden meaning for
one versed in prophecy; for if night closes
his eyes in death, this boasting image will
be fitting for the bearer of it when he falls,
its insolence an augury of his end.
As combatant to defend the gate and to engage
Tydeus I will send Melanippus, shrewd
son of Astacus, nobly born, who hates
all haughty talk; a retiring man, but quick—   440
no coward he!—when honor calls for action;
model of modesty, sprout of heroes that Ares
once spared: thus truly one of us, the sown men!
Though Ares will decide the outcome with his dice,
he stands to win through kinship to Justice—to keep
the spear from her who brought him into the world.
(Exit Melanippus.)

CHORUS *(in unison)*

May the gods make our man
the winner, since with right
on his side he goes to defend
our city; yet I look   450
aghast on blood to be shed
by those who fall for their kin.

SCOUT

May the gods grant him success! Now Capaneus
by lot is posted to the Electran gate,
another giant, taller indeed than Tydeus
but, like him, boasts with more than human pride
and hurls grave threats against our fortress heights.
And swears, whether the gods assist or hinder,

to scale the ramparts and make havoc of
our beleaguered city; even the bolt of Zeus,   460
should it fall from heaven to the plain where he
advances, will not block his way. The god's
thunder and lightning he compares to the sun
and heat of noon. He bears a vile device—
one man, naked, bearing in his hands
only a lighted torch; in golden letters
a caption reads, *I Come To Burn Your Town.*
What combatant will you send to cope with him,
who can withstand those vaunts unflinchingly?

ETEOCLES
Here's welcome word to add to our good news!   470
His coat of arms bodes well for us; the truth
will give the lie to such gross vanity!
Capaneus' incautious mouth dishonors heaven,
his wild euphoria, a fool's; for he
is only human and his inflated bluster
will reach the ears of Zeus. And I am certain
Zeus' flaming thunderbolt will find him out
and will be nothing like the heat of noontide.
Against him and his boastful mouth I send
the stalwart Polyphontes, whose spirit burns   480
for glory, reliable guard by grace of Artemis
and the other powers.
(Exit Polyphontes.)
                              Now tell me the next who has
been posted to yet another of our gates.

CHORUS
May the proud man who struts,
the big talker, who rants
against the city, perish.
May heaven strike him dead
with lightning before he forces

my abode and tears me
from my girlhood bower   490
with his imperious spear!

SCOUT

Now I will tell you who has drawn the lot
to be the third attacking our gates. To the hand
of Eteoclus the lot flew from an upturned helmet,
bronze vessel of Fortune, bidding him
to the Neistian gate, there to marshal his troops.
He draws up his chariots, horses neighing in harness,
eager for action; their snaffles ring, shaken
by snorting nostrils. On his shield another ensign
of showy pride: an armed assailant swarms up   500
a scaling ladder to a battlement
manned by his foe; the way he looks, success
will be his. He cries (and so the legend reads),
Not Even Ares Should Cast Me from the Bulwarks.
Do send a worthy warrior to ward off this man
and the yoke of slavery he would place on Thebes.
(*Exit Megareus.*)

ETEOCLES

In fact, I will send this man here, wishing him
good fortune. Indeed, I see he's gone already:
Megareus, ready with deeds not words, the son
of Creon, whose kin descend from earth that Cadmus   510
sowed with the dragon's teeth. He'll not retreat
from madly snorting steeds; either he'll die
paying his debt to the land that nurtured him
or he will slay Eteoclus and strip him—
his armor, and the shield depicting both the men
and the city—taking them home to hang as trophies
on his father's wall. Now tell who is next, and don't
spare me the whole story of his boasting.

CHORUS

> Godspeed, success be with you,
> defender of our homes!   520
> May these vainglorious braggarts
> who fling outrageous boasts
> against our city fall
> in harm's way; and Zeus, hearing
> their rant, look down in wrath
> and give their pride a jolt.

SCOUT

> Another challenger, the fourth, with noisy
> bravado, massively built Hippomedon
> stands by the gate adjoining Onca Athena;
> and I must say I shivered when he brandished   530
> the great round of his shield. No ordinary
> smith had worked the symbols on that circle;
> the design shows Typhon from his fiery mouth
> spewing forth black smoke, sister of fire.
> And round the hollowed shield's circumference runs
> a wreath of snakes that writhe and twine. The man
> himself brazens his menace out, possessed
> by Ares, raving for war like a maenad. Such
> madness calls for a strong defense—a rout
> starts soon, and Panic stands hard by the gate.   540

ETEOCLES

> First, Pallas, who (called Onca) lives enshrined
> outside the city near that gate and who
> despises a cheeky man, will hold him off,
> guarding her brood as from a lurking snake.
> Hyperbius, then, the stalwart son of Oenops—
> blameless in person, spirit, or readiness
> in arms—I choose to grapple man to man
> with this fellow, for he is bent on finding

the destiny fate has in store for him
today. In skillful Hermes' lottery   550
they are fairly matched, for each is ravenous
for combat with the other; to join their shields,
engaging the hostile gods depicted there:
on one, the fire-breathing Typhon, while
Hyperbius shows father Zeus on the other,
lightning bolt in hand, whom no one yet
saw conquered. Such is the aid and comfort friends
among the gods can give; we will be victors
and they will be the conquered here—that is,
if Zeus should conquer Typhon. But just as he   560
will surely triumph, by far the greater force
than Typhon, Zeus with his charged bolt saving
Hyperbius—so the men who struggle there
will fare as do their guardian deities.
(Exit Hyperbius.)

CHORUS

I trust he will fall, who bears
on his shield an earthling god
hated by Zeus, born not
of heaven but of earth,
whose likeness is despised
by men and gods at once.   570
Death will befall him. Death
will behead him at our gate.

SCOUT

So may it be! Now I'll describe the fifth,
deployed at the fifth and northerly gate, by the tomb
of Amphion, son of Zeus. He swears, by the spear
he carries like an amulet and prizes
more than gods or his own eyes, that he
will sack the Cadmeans' city in spite of Zeus.
Such is the vow of the son, fair pride of a mother

from the mountains, only a soldiering lad whose beard   580
but now on downy cheeks begins to darken
their ingenuous blush. With heart unlike
his face, or the woman's name his name includes,
he comes with ruthless look and brutal heart.
He flaunts as well a boast before the gate,
a shield of bronze, curved bastion for his body,
bright with an image of the man-eating Sphinx,
the shame of Thebes, gleaming in beaten bronze,
secured with studs; beneath her she pins a man,
a Cadmean spreadeagled, exposed to take   590
any weapon we let fly. This game-cock comes
as if he means to stay in business; not
for a visit, having come from far Arcadia;
by name, Parthenopaeus, an itinerant
who proposes here to pay his debt to Argos—
his adopted home—for hospitality and nurture,
by threatening and soon by ravaging
our battlements—I pray the gods prevent him
from making good his threats to ravage us!

ETEOCLES

May they themselves receive what they have promised—   600
from the gods. Because of these most blasphemous
tirades, you may be sure that they will perish
utterly. For this one too, for your Arcadian,
we have a match; no braggart, but a man
who knows his job: Actor, brother of him
just named. He'll let no inexperienced lad,
however blustering—bearing that odious beast
upon his buckler—force our gate; but the Sphinx
with whom he threatens us shall turn on him
who carries her against us, when she is   610
battered and smashed beneath our Theban walls.
May it please the gods, what I speak here is truth!
(*Exit Actor.*)

CHORUS

> The words of your scout have pierced me,
> they drill into my heart.
> It makes my hackles rise
> to hear such blasphemy,
> such braggart shrill descant
> from that desecrating gang.
> May the gods destroy them who
> would violate my land.   620

SCOUT

> I come at last to the sixth, a man well chosen
> for valor and even temper, a seer himself,
> the mighty Amphiaraus. Already holding
> the Homoloean gate, he rails at great Tydeus,
> accusing him of murder as being the chief
> author of evil in Argos, and plots against
> the state; henchman of fate; agent of slaughter;
> Adrastus' prompter in foul stratagems.
> Then, alluding to your father's fate,
> he calls on your own brother, strong Polynices;   630
> shuffles the parts of the name, putting the last
> half first; toys with the name, troubles your brother;
> reproaches him thus: "Will what we do here please
> the gods, make a tale worth telling: to raze your father's
> city and its gods; sack it with foreign arms?
> How will the gaining of a legal claim
> make good the shedding of so much blood and tears?
> How shall the fatherland you sprang from, that now
> a sword makes yours, join with you; fight by your side?
> For me, I'll fertilize your soil with this,   640
> my flesh, a seer interred in a foreign land.
>   Onward!
> I welcome battle—no degrading fate awaits me."
> So spoke the prophet, serene, and raised his shield.

No heraldry emblazoned it, for he would not
appear, but *be*: intending excellence
not pretense—while he gathered from the folds
of his mind the fruits from which his wisdom came.
So: you had better send antagonists
both shrewd and fierce to counter him. Whoever
truly worships the gods is someone to fear.   650

ETEOCLES
Alas, for this sign that seems to link the true
believer with the blasphemous. A cabal
with evil men is the worst scenario. The fruits
of such fellowship should not be harvested.
A good man, shipped with sailors bent on piracy,
may suffer with that criminal crew; go down
with the ungodly. Or a righteous man, who falls
among vile men who violate the rites
of hospitality and disregard the gods,
may go down, caught with them; laid low by a god,   660
by the same blow that falls on all alike.
Now this seer, Oecles' son—a moderate
and pious man, just and benevolent,
reliable prophet—against his better judgment
sided with sacrilegious men who led
this long march against us, and with them shall
be smashed to pieces by the power of Zeus.
Indeed, my guess would be he'll not attack us,
not out of cowardice or lack of spirit, but
knowing he'll die in battle, if the oracles   670
of Loxias Apollo—one known to hold his tongue
until the time is fitting—are borne out.
Nevertheless, we commission his opponent:
muscular Lasthenes, gatekeeper who does not follow
the ways of hospitality; the wisdom of age
in a body brimming with strength of youth, an eye

that sprints and hand as quick with spear to take
whatever is left unguarded by the shield.
                                        And yet
when a man wins, it is the gift of the gods.
(Exit Lasthenes.)

CHORUS

O gods, hear us; listen   680
to our righteous prayers!
May it come to pass that the city
has good luck. Turn the sword
that threatens to end our people
on the invader. May Zeus,
driving them back, strike them
dead outside the walls.

SCOUT

Now I will tell you of the seventh, him
assigned to the seventh gate, what he desires
at the hands of the gods, what curses he calls down   690
upon the city.
                    And this is your blood brother!
He announces that either he will mount our wall
shouting the victory-cry at our submission
and be proclaimed our lord, meeting you there
and cutting you down; or die himself beside you;
or, if both survive, to be revenged
by banishing you, who banished him, making
you pay with exile: as you have made him pay!
        Great Polynices clamors with these threats
and prays to the gods of his hearth to make them good.   700
He bears a brand-new shield, it gleams as he moves
and sports a double image, apt for this
venture. A ladylike woman leads a man
in arms, and both in beaten gold. She claims

to be Justice, and her motto reads, "I lead
this man back to his city, where he shall rule
and dwell in the house of his fathers."
                                        Such are his
slogans and devices! Now you decide
who goes. Pray, don't blame me for the news I bring:
you are Thebes' guide and pilot in this storm.   710
(Exit Scout.)

ETEOCLES
O family, godforsaken, still god-hated,
cursed line of Oedipus!
                            I thought in my case
Apollo would relent. But no! The curse
of my father comes to fix me, skewer my heart!

Yet this is not the hour to wail; my tears
may generate a greater grief. Now—
as for Polynices—soon enough events
will show how true the emblem on his shield
turns out to be, and if those gilded words,
swollen with rash drivel and mad delusion,   720
shall bring him what he wants. If Justice, pure
daughter of Zeus, had moved him in his thoughts
and deeds, this outcome might have come to pass.
But never in his life, from the shade of infancy,
to the green vigor of boyhood, until the beard
of manhood began to gather on his chin,
did Justice deem him fit or show him favor.
Nor is it likely she will now support him
when he would fall upon his fatherland.
Indeed, Justice would not be just if she   730
allied herself with that demented mind.
Secure in this knowledge, I will take him on;
who more fitting than I? Foe with foe,

captain confronting captain, brother against
brother, I go to meet him. Bring my greaves,
my armor, gear to fend off spears and arrows.

CHORUS
Precious child of Oedipus,
do not be carried away
by rank fever for war
like him of harrowing name!   740
Hard enough that Cadmeans
close with Argives in battle;
for such bloodshed atonement
may come, but not for blood
among brothers, pollution
that sends roots down and thrives.

ETEOCLES
If evil visits a good man, so be it;
that is no dishonor. Only the dead
are free of woe. But as for glory, when
misfortune and dishonor join as one,   750
no worthy fame results.
(begins to put on his armor)

CHORUS
                          My son, why so relentless?
Do not let wrathful lust, shaking the spear,
overwhelm you; rather banish that first,
impulsive response.

ETEOCLES
                          Since the god presses the issue,
let the entire clan of Laius—abhorrent
to Apollo—drive, sail, before the wind
down to the tearful waters of Cocytus!

CHORUS

> This bestial lusting after unlawful blood
> gnaws at you, eats at you, carries you on to do
> a savage deed—the shedding of a man's   760
> blood, the fruit of which makes bitter harvest.

ETEOCLES

> Oh, yes, the damnable curse of my beloved
> father is fulfilled! It roosts beside me
> with staring eyes unweeping, telling me
> how triumph shall precede my certain doom.

(buckles on sword)

CHORUS

> Yet do not hasten it! You'll not be called
> a coward if you, with honor, save your skin.
> The storm-cloud that enfolds stern Erinys
> will spare your land, pass by your dwelling, if
> she receives a fitting sacrifice from your hands.   770

ETEOCLES

> For some time now indeed we've gone neglected
> by the gods! Or with a cold eye they notice—
> taking their pleasure in our self-destruction—
> and welcome the offering with which we perish.
> Why kneel to Fate when sentenced to death already?

CHORUS

> No, take advantage of the time you have. The gods
> may be slow, but they may yet change course; the gale
> of Fate may fall to a gentle breeze, though now
> it rages.

ETEOCLES

> Rage? The curses of Oedipus still
> breathe fire and fury; all too true, my nightmares   780
> foretelling division of our father's estate!

(finishes arming, picks up shield)

CHORUS
     Be ruled by women, however you may scold us.

ETEOCLES
     Speak, then, what you will, but make it quick.

CHORUS

                                             In a word,
     do not go on this way—to the seventh gate.

ETEOCLES
     Set as I am on going, words won't stop me.

CHORUS
     Gods smile on victory even if won with caution.

ETEOCLES
     No warrior could take such an adage seriously!

CHORUS
     But shed your brother's blood? Can you mean it?
     Surely you would not—

ETEOCLES
                         To whom the gods
     would bring destruction, destruction surely comes.   790
     (Exit Eteocles.)

FIRST PAIR OF CHORISTERS
     I tremble now, fearing the power
     of the goddess, she who lays waste homes,
     ruin that hovers near us now.
     Called up by curses of the father,
     the Erinyes, brooding on evil, bring
     to a head the wrathful maledictions

spoken by crazed Oedipus
against his very children, his stock.
This is the scion-destroying strife,
born of a father's rage, that has   800
aroused her to follow at close range.

SECOND PAIR OF CHORISTERS
    A Scythian stranger, alien out of
Chalybia, harsh partitioner
with blade of sternly tempered steel,
portions out a family's riches,
to each his destined plot of land.
Unjustly stripped of heritage,
the rich are denied landed estates,
each paltry lot no more than that
six feet he'll occupy in death.   810

THIRD PAIR OF CHORISTERS
    When each has been butchered
by the other's arms, brother murdering brother,
    and both have fallen; when
the dust of the earth shall have drunk their black blood,
    who will there be for them,
to bathe them, purify their bodies, perform
    the proper rites for them?
O fresh disasters, mixing with the ancient
    agonies of this family!

FIRST PAIR OF CHORISTERS
    I speak of that original   820
transgression and its timely punishment
    posterity ever since
has mourned: three generations now have borne
    its weight, despite Apollo's
promise three times made at the Pythian oracle,
    that if King Laius died

childless, he would save his kingdom. But
    Laius, sunk in lust,

fathered his own demise:
King Oedipus who sowed the awful seed   830
    in hallowed ground, the womb
where he had gotten life; then grew, returning
    to plant a bloody root;
Oedipus, the parricide; and Jocasta, unlucky
    couple yoked by lust!

SECOND PAIR OF CHORISTERS
    Misfortunes are like a sea
on which, when one wave falls, another surges,
    tripling the crest of the swell
before, each beating harder upon the ship
    of the city, whose wooden hull   840
is a frail fence only, no defense against
    the ravages of the sea.
I fear that Thebes and all her kings will capsize,
    toppled by such battering.

THIRD PAIR OF CHORISTERS
    And when the time comes round at last
    the venerable curse must be fulfilled;
    payment due with interest; ruin,
    once on board, invincibly plunders
    the hard-won goods that merchants stowed
    so proudly, casting them overboard.   850

No one was more admired or
honored than Oedipus was once,
whether by gods or citizens
of the city, or even countryfolk.
Oedipus who once had banished

from the realm the Sphinx, the plague
that throttled men across the land.

FIRST PAIR OF CHORISTERS
    But when he roused himself
and learned at last how woeful his disastrous
        wedlock was, despairing   860
in his pain, distracted by a heart gone mad,
        he worked a double crime.
His father-murdering hand clawed up amok
        against his eyes, more dear
to him than his sweet children; clawed his eyes out.

    Outraged to feel the pains
of thirst and hunger, he lashed out against
        his sons with words remorse
might not reprieve, the curse—that they at some point
        yet to come, brandishing   870
bright swords, should cut in two his land and his
        estate. Fear makes me tremble,
now that Erinys—the swiftest sprinter—
        will make this come to pass.
(*Enter Scout.*)

SCOUT
    All of you, every tender daughter raised
by her mother, cheer up now; for Thebes has crushed
the relentless enemy and quelled its rant.
We are delivered from defeat and bondage.
The city is becalmed; it shipped no water,
sprang no leak, though battered by so many   880
menacing waves. Our battlements stood firm
with heroes, masters in hand-to-hand combat,
shielding every portal—all but one.
All has gone well at six gates but, at the seventh,

where our revered lord chose himself to go,
Apollo has thought to bring to pass judgment
on the kin of Oedipus, thus to close the book
on Laius' awful folly long ago.

CHORUS *(in unison)*
What comes to pass, afflicting our city now?

SCOUT
Two princes fall, each by the other's hand—   890

CHORUS
What are you saying—of whom do you speak?
I quake at the prospect of fresh news.

SCOUT
                              Calm down;
control yourself! Listen to me. The progeny
of Oedipus—

CHORUS
                    Gods, I am so wretched; and I
foretold these evils!

SCOUT
                    Both of them ate the dust,
no doubt of that.

CHORUS
                    Ah, this is too much.
Did it come to that?
                    —Go on . . . out there, you say?

SCOUT
Both men lie dead, each murdered by the other.

CHORUS

    Then with a brother's hands did each undo
    the other, fate even-handed to the last?   900

SCOUT

    Just so. Their destinies identical, the fate
    of one that of the other; in one stroke
    oblivion enveloped their doomed clan.
    Thus we must weep and celebrate at once,
    for Thebes is free of that foul destiny.
    Yet we shed tears for her most stalwart leaders,
    heroic men who thus divided their
    estate with hammer-tempered Scythian iron.
    Now each comes into but the land his grave
    takes up, done in by a father's curse. Thebes   910
    is free, but the earth of the homeland drinks the blood
    of her two princes, born of one seed, and dead.
(Exit Scout.)

CHORUS

    Omnipotent Zeus, and guardian
    spirits of the city who
    steadfast have held our Cadmean
    bastion impregnable, should
    I raise triumphal song
    for the clean victory we
    have won? Or weep and mourn
    for those fraternal princes   920
    now lost, star-crossed, sterile,
    never to father sons?
    In truth, just as both
    their names implied—the sense
    of each, *Correctly Named*;
    and both, *Abundant Strife*—
    through haughty ways they have fallen
    with their ungodly goals.

FIRST PAIR OF CHORISTERS
    O dark curse of the father,
on all his issue, now fulfilled, the curse   930
    of Oedipus: in terror
the blood in my veins goes sluggish, cold; my heart
    is thumping! Like a crazed
maenad, when I hear of their slain bodies
    dribbling with gore, and how
those two in combat met one cruel doom,
    I make funereal keening
for the harsh music of two clashing spears.

SECOND PAIR OF CHORISTERS
    The anathema of the father
has come about and run its course; the schemes   940
    of unbelieving Laius
have won out, surrounding us with anguish.
    I fear for the city, since
prescriptions of the gods retain full potency.
(Funeral procession enters with two bodies on biers, carried on the
    shoulders of bearers.)
    You who bring us double
sorrow, you have perpetrated this
    horrible deed, which passes
comprehension, and yet fresh miseries
    still throng and hem us in!
It is clear to me now. The tale the sentinel told   950
    is here before my eyes.
Our pains are doubled, doubled our dreadful griefs.
    What shall I say? What more?
That sorrows never come singly and have for long
    resided in this house?

THIRD PAIR OF CHORISTERS
    Come, friends, our manifold
lamentations must begin; raise up

your arms and thrash your hands;
with stately measure beat them against your heads,
    which, with our gale of cries,   960
will guide the soundless, sacred, black-sailed ship
    freighted with death across
the river Acheron to the sunless land
    where Apollo never treads,
invisible shore that must admit all men.
(Enter Antigone and Ismene. The bearers put down the biers of Polynices
and Eteocles, then stand aside.)

CHORUS LEADER
    Enough.
    Here come Ismene and Antigone
    to do their duty,
    appalling office, burial of their brothers.
    I've no doubt they'll give,   970
    from the bottom of their hearts,
    appropriate wails
    deep from their ample breasts.
    But first we'll raise
    the awe-inspiring chant of the Erinyes,
    and then we'll sing the hateful anthem of Hades.
    O dearest ones!
    Least fortunate of women,
    those of close-cinched robes,
    dear sisters of such brothers,   980
    I will mourn for you. I grieve for you,
    cries straight from the heart.

THIRD PAIR OF CHORISTERS
    I pity you, perverse young men
    who trust no friend, whom evil deeds
    have not tripped up; you moved against
    your father's hall with spear held high.

CHORUS LEADER
>Wretched in truth are they who found
>death in the ruin they brought their house.

FIRST PAIR OF CHORISTERS, WITH ANTIGONE
>O brothers who would overcome
>the palace you were born in; scale   990
>its walls and topple them, who eyed
>the spiteful throne itself, have you
>settled your claims at last with the sword?

SECOND PAIR OF CHORISTERS, WITH ISMENE
>How well the Erinys of Oedipus
>has made a father's will come true.

FIRST PAIR OF CHORISTERS, WITH ANTIGONE
>Each wounded on his left side, indeed,
>run through by a brother's right-hand blow,
>strange bodies born from a single womb,
>what a curse that called down blow for blow!

SECOND PAIR OF CHORISTERS, WITH ISMENE
>Pierced clean through they were, as you say;   1000
>their bodies and their family name
>wasted by rage and the fate decreed
>by the father's curse, a fate they shared
>for once with brotherly accord.

FIRST PAIR OF CHORISTERS, WITH ANTIGONE
>Still, grief steps everywhere in the city,
>it shrouds the towers, baffles the fields;
>while riches that caused the strife and garnered
>death remain for those who live.

SECOND PAIR OF CHORISTERS, WITH ISMENE
>With fired hearts they divided up
>their estate in equal portions; yet   1010

their friends will blame the judge, and Ares,
who differed—and gave them miserable war.

FIRST PAIR OF CHORISTERS, WITH ANTIGONE
　　By bloodshed they have come to this,
　　and bloodshed awaits them in the tombs.
　　How so, you ask? Ancestral blood
　　the fathers shed is with them in the grave.

SECOND PAIR OF CHORISTERS, WITH ISMENE
　　From deep within, loud groans enfold
　　us all; wailings of grief, the pain
　　of joyless, suffering minds weeping
　　uncontrollably from the soul.   1020

　　With cries that rise from a broken heart
　　I watch the funeral train pass by.

FIRST PAIR OF CHORISTERS, WITH ANTIGONE
　　Now we can say these wretched men
　　brought us great pain and harmed the state,
　　and harmed those others, ally or enemy,
　　who perished in this senseless war.

SECOND PAIR OF CHORISTERS, WITH ISMENE
　　No mother more unfortunate
　　than she who bore these boys, oh, none
　　more doomed among all women, so
　　many as are mothers on this earth.   1030

　　Ill-fated, she took her very son
　　for husband, then gave birth to these
　　who took their lives by their own hands,
　　two sons who gave each other death.

FIRST PAIR OF CHORISTERS, WITH ANTIGONE
　　In truth they were brotherly in death!
　　Undone by a hostile severing of

fraternal bonds, they madly fought
till fratricide resolved their feud.

SECOND PAIR OF CHORISTERS, WITH ISMENE
Their mutual hatred's done its work.
On the shambles of their dueling ground   1040
their life-blood mingles in earth. So they
are one blood now! The whetted blade

from overseas, a referee
well tempered from the forge, has ruled;
dark Ares, sharp apportioner
of shares, made good the father's vow.

FIRST PAIR OF CHORISTERS, WITH ANTIGONE
Miserable youths! Their legacy
is heaven-sent afflictions. The deep
and fathomless extent of earth
beneath their graves is all their wealth.   1050

Oh, how you left your family
festooned with ills! And when it fell
the throng of curses screamed their cry.
Now all the members of your house

run for their lives. On the gate where they
attacked each other, Destruction, who
undid them both, has hung a garland;
and that demonic force subsides.
(Antigone and Ismene move to stand by the biers of Polynices and
Eteocles.)

CHORUS LEADER
When you were wounded, you would strike again.

SECOND CHORISTER
When you dealt death, you died yourself.

THIRD CHORISTER

You killed   1060

by the spear.

FOURTH CHORISTER

And by the spear you fell.

FIFTH CHORISTER

What you did

was hell on earth.

SIXTH CHORISTER

Your suffering was your hell.

CHORUS LEADER

Go ahead, let tears come.

SECOND CHORISTER

Cry, and groan out loud.

THIRD CHORISTER

You're leveled now—

FOURTH CHORISTER

though you laid low!

FIFTH CHORISTER

Laid out

for burial, ah!

SIXTH CHORISTER

Oh, yes.

ANTIGONE

Ah me, my heart

is crazed.

ISMENE

Deep in my bosom my heart groans.

ANTIGONE

O brother, you deserve my lamentation!

ISMENE

And you—utterly deserving.

ANTIGONE

You died at the hand of a beloved brother.

ISMENE

With your hand you killed a loved one and a brother.   1070

ANTIGONE

Double terrors to report.

ISMENE

And their twins
to look upon.

ANTIGONE

These awful slaughters are
cousin to such miseries.

ISMENE

The brother's
sorrow is housed next door to a sister's grief.

CHORUS *(in unison)*

Ah, Fate, whose legatees inherit trouble
and you, dread ghost of Oedipus, and Erinys,
black as midnight: truly you have great might.

ANTIGONE
 Oh, me.

ISMENE
        And me.

ANTIGONE
             Heartaches hard to look at—

ISMENE
 such as he told of when he came from exile.

ANTIGONE
 Yet there was no salvation after slaughter.   1080

ISMENE
 Yes, but when he was saved already, he died.

ANTIGONE
 You say it, he lost his life.

ISMENE
                    And he cut down
 his brother.

ANTIGONE
          Oh, my family, damned—

ISMENE
                         that knows
 misery. So many woes that have one name!

CHORUS *(in unison)*
 Alas, O Fate, who portions out disaster,
 and you, dread ghost of Oedipus, and Erinys,
 black as midnight: truly you have great might.

ANTIGONE

>You know all this because you have been through it!

ISMENE

>And so do you, learning it just as soon
>as he—

ANTIGONE

>   after you came home to Thebes,   1090

ISMENE

>to meet this man in combat with your spear.

ANTIGONE

>Talk of annihilation—

ISMENE

>   and look upon it!

ANTIGONE

>Oh! Such disaster!

ISMENE

>   Terrible outcome for—

ANTIGONE

>our family, our state—

ISMENE

>   and, most, for me.

ANTIGONE

>As much or more for me.

FIRST PAIR OF CHORISTERS

>   I pity this pain,
>your wretchedness, O lord Eteocles,
>our chief!

SECOND PAIR OF CHORISTERS
Pity on you both, you two
most miserable of men!

THIRD PAIR OF CHORISTERS
Deranged by fate!
(A pause, as Antigone walks distractedly upstage.)

ANTIGONE
Ah me! Where ever shall we bury them?

ISMENE
In the most honored place—

ANTIGONE
the holiest plot.   1100
Fit misery fit to lie beside their father!
(Enter Herald.)

HERALD
It is for me now to announce the pleasure
of the council of Thebes and their decree.
They do resolve to give
(gestures to first bier)
this body here,
Eteocles, for his great dedication
to the state, interment in this earth,
the precious sepulcher of Cadmean soil.
For he has not offended holy fanes,
has died as a youthful patriot ought to die,
repelling enemies of his native place.   1110
So much am I required to speak of him.
But as for this,
(moves to the second bier)
the corpse of Polynices,
our leader's brother, inasmuch as he—
if a certain god had not stepped in to guide

his brother's spear—would have overturned
the city and laid waste our Cadmean realm:
he shall be cast beyond the gates, unburied,
a meal for dogs. Though he is dead already
he must bear the curse of his homeland's gods,
for he dishonored them, polluting his   1120
city with invasion by a foreign power.
Therefore it is resolved that he will lie
without honor, to be picked apart by seabirds,
his sundered body borne aloft and thus
dispersed on the winds. Thus will he receive
a just reward; and no one is to raise
a burial mound or keen with loud laments.
No funeral will honor him. Such is
the verdict of the Theban government.

ANTIGONE

No Theban council has jurisdiction here!   1130
I must respond to the Cadmean rulers thus:
if no one other than myself is willing
to join with me and give him decent burial,
I will do these things and bury him myself.
Regardless of consequences I will take
the risk of opposing the authorities
and bury my brother. In doing this duty
I find it no shame to disobey the state.
Blood-ties, the kinship of a common womb
and the same ill-fated parents, these are more   1140
powerful than your decrees. Now then,
my soul, with your own free will, we will share
these wrongs heaped on the dead, though he would never
wish such sisterly spirit. Mind you, no
ravening wolves will rip and gnaw his flesh—
let someone try to *order* that! While I
am here, though only a woman, I will dig
a grave and build a tomb for him, and if

I have to, carry in the folds of my linen robe
armfuls of earth for him. Let no one doubt me!   1150
Be bold my heart, courage will find a way.

HERALD

You are forbidden to act in such a manner;
you must not take Thebes' law
into your own hands.

ANTIGONE

I command you not to speak. You waste your breath.

HERALD

After such a brush with disaster, Thebes
will be ruthless.

ANTIGONE

Ruthless is it? But
a burial there will be.

HERALD

What are you saying?
Whom the city casts out, you would raise up?

ANTIGONE

Long ago the gods had stopped protecting him.   1160

HERALD

Not so, they honored him till he attacked
our homeland.

ANTIGONE

He was done injury and
gave injury in return.

HERALD

He alone was harmed,
the harm he did caused harm to everyone.

ANTIGONE

The last god to be still is Disagreement.
I go to bury him. Not another word
from you!

HERALD

So. Have it your way then. I still forbid you!
(Exit Herald.)

FIRST PAIR OF CHORISTERS

Ah! The ruinous strength of fate, the scourge
of families, has struck the stock of Laius,   1170
torn up the line of Oedipus by the roots.
What shall I do? What counsel shall I take,
what badge shall I put on? Must I not weep
for you as well and join the line of mourners
following to the tomb? But fears accost me,
the anger of the people frightens me.
You will have many mourners, Eteocles,
but he, your brother, will have few, or none.
He goes unwept, but for a sister's tears
that follow him, a solitary dirge.   1180
O desperate dead, will you agree with this?

SECOND PAIR OF CHORISTERS

Let the state do what it will,
punish or pardon those who must
weep for him, the brother. Poor
Polynices! As for us,
we will now escort him and
join the sad procession. Both
family and city own

the grief for this sad death;
states that act by popular will   1190
may, in good time, change course still.

THIRD PAIR OF CHORISTERS
But we walk with this other bier
as Justice, and the people too,
require. For with the aid of Zeus
and other blissful gods, this man,
Eteocles, our foremost man,
preserved the Cadmean city from
a tidal wave, the invading foe;
from being scuttled by a war,
unthinkable calamity.   1200

(*The choristers divide; half exit with Ismene and the bier of Eteocles stage
left, half with Antigone and the bier of Polynices,
stage right.*)

The Suppliants

Translated by
Gail Holst-Warhaft

Translator's Preface

Some ancient plays need very little introduction; they present themselves to us with such dramatic force and tell their own stories so clearly, even in a pedestrian translation, that they seem independent of their time and place. Aeschylus' *Suppliants* is not a play like this. In fact most modern commentators have been puzzled as to why it was included in the selection of seven Aeschylean tragedies made sometime in late antiquity, and so preserved in the various manuscript copies handed down to us. Very little happens in *The Suppliants*. The play is one long argument; its principal speakers are not characters, in the modern sense, but a group of young women whose opposition to a marriage arranged with their cousins is radical and adamant. Was it preserved for its ideas, expressed largely in the successfully persuasive arguments of the Danaids? Or was for the beauty of Aeschylus' poetry and the music we can never hear? Probably it was preserved for both these reasons, making the translator's task doubly difficult. It is tremendously important, in a play of ideas, where the ground shifts constantly and each point is won by rhetoric, to make the argument as clear as it must have been to its original audience. But it is equally important to remember that what is said is not prose but poetry, and was not only spoken but at least partly sung. If translation is to give any impression of the operatic richness of the original, it must be in a metrical form that makes sense of the dense and supple Greek; it must point up the difference between a sung chorus and a swift exchange of dialogue, and at the same time allow the reader to think about the issues raised by the play, issues as relevant to today's world as they were to Aeschylus'.

There is some background information a reader needs to know if he or she is to follow the argument of *The Suppliants*. The play was once part of a tetralogy of three tragedies and a satyr play, all based on the legend of the Danaids and their refusal to marry their cousins. *The Suppliants* seems to have been the first of the three tragedies. Almost all that we know of the second play is its title, *The Aegyptiads*. Of the third tragedy, *The Danaids*, a few small fragments remain, and they tell us very little about the way Aeschylus concluded his trilogy. The satyr play that followed was called *Amymone*. Its central character was one of the Danaids, and its farcical humor was derived from the frustration of the satyrs who tried to seduce her.

Whether or not Aeschylus invented many of the details of the legend of the Danaids to suit his purpose we will never know, but the story of the reluctant brides and their cousins was an old one and some features of the legend remain constant in the various versions. We must presume that an audience of Aeschylus' contemporaries would have been familiar with the outline of the story, and so would have known, from the beginning, what fate lay in store for the Aegyptiads. If we are to understand the extreme aversion of the Danaids to marriage and the violence of their rhetoric, we, too, need to know more than the first play tells us. Here, then, is the story of the daughters of Danaus, cobbled together from the sources we have.

It begins with Danaus, a powerful lord or king of Libya or Egypt, and his brother Aegyptus, who is in one version the ruler of Arabia. Danaus and his fifty daughters flee from Egypt. According to some versions their flight is either because of a quarrel between the two brothers or because Danaus is told by an oracle that a marriage between his daughters and the Aegyptiads will endanger his life. In Aeschylus' version, the Danaids initiate the flight simply because they cannot bear the thought of marrying their cousins. They arrive safely in Argos with the help of Athena. Aegyptus orders his sons not to return from Argos until they have killed Danaus. Already, as the action of *The Suppliants* begins, Aeschylus' version differs in some points from other sources, but the essential ingredients are in place: the flight from Egypt to Argos, the refusal of marriage, the complicity of the father in the daughters' escape, the pursuit of the Danaids by the Aegyptiads. In Aeschylus' version the Danaids argue their right to protection on the grounds of their Argive ancestry. Io, their great-grandmother, was an Argive priestess of Hera with whom Zeus fell in love. Charged by his furious wife with infidelity, Zeus turned Io into a white cow that Hera claimed as hers and set the many-eyed Argus to guard. With Hermes' help, Zeus managed to free Io, but Hera set a gadfly to chase her, and Io fled her tormenter, running a long and tortuous course through Asia Minor and Europe before coming to rest in Egypt. There Zeus found her and begat a child by breathing on and touching her. The child's name, Epaphus, reflected his magical birth. Epaphus was the father of Danaus and Aegyptus.

The Suppliants ends with the decision of Pelasgus, King of Argos, to protect his Egyptian kin, even if it means war with their cousins. The sources are in some disagreement about what follows. Danaus, according to most versions, becomes king of Argos and is besieged by Aegyptus and his sons. In Aeschylus' trilogy there appears to have been a war between the Aegyptiads and the Argives. An offer of reconciliation is made and Danaus agrees to marry his daughters to Aegyptus' sons, but he orders them to kill their bridegrooms on the wedding night. All the daughters except Hypermestra carry out their task. Either because he respects her virginity or because she falls in love with him, Hypermestra spares her husband, Lynceus. Lynceus flees to Lyrceia and Danaus keeps Hypermestra locked up, Aegyptus arrives to avenge the murder of his sons, and Lynceus, some say, mediates between his father and Danaus. Athena and Hermes purify the Danaids; Hypermestra and Lynceus are reunited. The remaining Danaids are married to Argives.

What are we to make of this story, and what are the issues it raises? The constants in all the variants of the Danaid legend are the refusal of marriage, the flight from Egypt to Greece, and the murder of the bridegrooms. Unless we know what violence the suppliant maidens are capable of, we are likely to miss the irony of their self-styled helplessness. Knowing it, we take their threat of suicide seriously. The Danaids are not simply opposed to this marriage; they are ready to die and to kill in order to avoid it. But why are they so opposed to it? And do they have any legal grounds for their objection? Do they hate marriage and sex in general, as some critics have argued, or is it this particular marriage that they find so repugnant? The most fascinating question of all is why Aeschylus gives such prominence to the feelings of the Danaids. In a society where marriages were automatically arranged and fathers were the ones who decided the future of their daughters, it is curious how little we hear from Danaus on the subject of his legal right to dispose of his daughters. In a series of speeches that seem peculiarly familiar and modern, the Danaids persuade Pelasgus that they cannot simply be handed over to men they detest because the marriage has been arranged. And if harboring these suppliants means war, Pelasgus is still prepared to defend them, whether or not he believes they have a legal leg to stand on.

The reason for Pelasgus' decision is not, I think, that he is impressed by the arguments of the suppliants about their feelings toward their prospective grooms. We must presume that the issues raised in this play, as in the other preserved works of Aeschylus, were neither eccentric nor trivial, and I'm afraid that the personal feelings of a group of young women toward their impending marriage would have seemed both to a contemporary audience. Some larger moral and philosophical question is at stake here, and it has to do with the Danaids' status as suppliants. The Danaids state clearly that they are personally responsible for their flight. They accuse their suitors of impiety and hubris, and claim that marriage to them would be equivalent to bondage, a claim that is substantiated by the behavior of the Aegyptiad herald, who treats them as runaway slaves and chattels of his masters, threatening them with violence if they resist. This may be a valid claim to a modern audience, but it must have carried little weight in the Athens of Aeschylus' day, and it carries none with Pelasgus. He tells them it is up to them to prove that the Aegyptiads have no control over them by Egyptian law.

What does carry weight with Pelasgus is the fact that the Danaids are suppliants at the Argive altars. For the argument between Pelasgus and the Danaids to have any dramatic tension, there must be some equality between the two sides. The Danaids appear, at first, to be a helpless group of young women. Pelasgus is king of a major Greek city. The young women seem to be in no position to bargain, and yet bargain they do, and the card they hold in their hands is strong enough to win their case. They begin by claiming kinship with Pelasgus through their Argive ancestress Io, but it is their relationship to Zeus through that union they intend to exploit. In their prayers to Zeus they use the same tactics as they do with Pelasgus. Zeus is mentioned 55 times in the play, more often than in any other play of Aeschylus, and usually with great respect, but the Danaids claim to a special relationship with him and so his obligation to protect them is pushed to the limit. Not only is he addressed as "Father" on a number of occasions and reminded of his wife's bad behavior to Io, but if he and the other Olympians fail to do their duty to their suppliant kin, the Danaids threaten to "supplicate" Hades by committing suicide. The threat is not idle, since they imagine Zeus will be subject to judgment in the underworld after his death:

> And if it should happen like this,
> won't Zeus be found guilty too,

he who disowns the child
he sired by a cow—his own son,
averting his eyes when we pray? (144–48)

The talk of suicide is echoed precisely in the Danaids' exchange with Pelasgus (425ff) where they threaten to hang themselves by their girdles from the images of the gods unless he gives in to their demands. It is their status as suppliants to the gods rather than their claim of Argive kinship that sways the king. Pelasgus is sufficiently afraid to anger Zeus in his capacity of god of suppliants, the "god whom mortals most fear," that he risks war on the Danaids' behalf.

Pelasgus and the city of Argos are won over by a combination of quasi-legal arguments put forward by the Danaids and of dire threats that, knowing the future history of the brides, we are prepared to take seriously. Legal terminology is frequently used, and Danaus gives his daughters advice like a trusted counsel. Around the outcrop of rock that dominated the city of Athens, the law courts, the assembly, and the theater of Dionysus not only were in physical proximity but shared an audience. It is not surprising that the vocabulary of one spilled over to the other, or that the same issues were explored in all three places. The chorus of Danaids plead their case with the skill of lawyers, the rhetoric of politicians, the dramatic pathos of tragic heroines. Their case for refusing marriage seems not to have been related to a particular event, nor to have any legal basis in Athenian law, under which fathers could dispose of their daughters as they wished. Why the Danaids should have been represented as having any say in choosing their husbands we can only imagine, but the fate awaiting the Aegyptiad bridegrooms makes it clear that thwarting the wishes of determined women involves a serious risk. It is a risk that a number of characters in Greek mythology ignore at their peril. More important than the arguments about the Danaids' distaste for marriage and their right to refuse it is the issue of sanctuary. It is a moral issue that the nations of the end of the twentieth century continue to grapple with in Bosnia, in Burundi, in Korea, along the Mexican border. To give sanctuary to refugees who claim they are being persecuted in their own country is often to risk armed conflict with the aggressor, but can a "civilized" country refuse sanctuary and not suffer the moral consequences? Will Zeus or any other god stand by and watch as the suppliants at his altar are dragged away?

It is this question that makes *The Suppliants* an enduring drama. In this century, we have passed moral judgment on many of the developed countries for their behavior toward suppliants. The nations who took in refugees, especially those who sheltered Jews during the Second World War, are looked on as examples of "good" nations. Those who didn't remain under a moral cloud. However distasteful the Danaids' future behavior, they have placed themselves in a position where a Greek king and his city have a moral duty toward them. Pelasgus' decision to respect the band of suppliant women gives him heroic stature; his magnanimous offer of hospitality, even in his own home, suggests that he has accepted the full weight of his obligations as host to the refugees, knowing it may cost him his city and his life.

NOTE ON THE SOURCES USED

The text of Aeschylus' *Suppliants* has been preserved in six manuscripts, all of which raise some problems because of erroneous corrections and additions. Modern editions of the play have skillfully sifted the evidence and arrived at conclusions that do not always agree. I have relied principally on the extensive apparatus of H. Friis Johansen and Edward W. Whittle.[1] I have followed their suggestion (2: 273) that the lacuna in lines 311–12 (338–39 of the transmitted text) probably consisted of a general statement by Pelasgus about husbands' rights over their wives irrespective of feelings and an objection by the leader of the chorus to his statement.

1. *Aeschylus: The Suppliants*, 3 vols., ed. H. Friis Johansen and Edward W. Whittle (Copenhagen: Gyldendalske Boghandel, Nordisk Forlag, 1980).

Cast

CHORUS OF DANAIDS
DANAUS
PELASGUS
EGYPTIAN HERALD
BODYGUARD
NONSPEAKING
    Maidservants
    Attendants to Pelasgus
    Attendants to herald

(The scene is a sanctuary on a high open space near the coast of
Argos. This is represented on a raised wooden stage. From the
sanctuary can be seen the sea in one direction and the city of
Argos in the other. There is an altar in the center along with
a number of larger-than-life images of the gods. In front of the
sanctuary, on the orchestra, is the level precinct to the sanctuary.
The chorus of Danaids, accompanied by their maidservants,
enter from the parados that represents the way to the sea.)

DANAIDS
    Protect us, God of Suppliants, Zeus!
    We sailed from the silty mouth of the Nile
    leaving behind your sacred lands
    that border Syria. We fled, not charged
    by the people's vote with a bloody crime,
    but, rather than face unholy marriage
    with Aegyptus' sons, we chose exile.
    Danaus, our father and adviser in chief,
    has played our game, decreeing flight
    the best of all evils; so we sailed   10
    and came to Argos, land of our race
    sprung from a gadfly-driven cow
    who conceived by Zeus' breath and touch.

What kinder land to come to than this,
with our suppliants' weapons, wool-wreathed branches?

Those to whom this city belongs,
its earth and clear water: the gods above,
vengeful gods of the tombs below,
and Zeus the Savior, who guards the homes
of righteous men, receive this band   20
of suppliant girls who reverently breathe
the air of this land. But as for that horde
of insolent men, sons of Aegyptus—
before they set foot on this swampy shore
with their quick-oared boat, send them back
to face the sea's rage. There may they die
in thunder and lightning, lashed by gales
under rain-soaked clouds before they climb
into unwilling beds, flaunting the law
that protects us and forcing cousins to wed.   30

Now I call
from beyond the sea
my divine helper
Zeus-sired calf,
son of my forebear
the flower-feasting cow:
conceived by his breath,
child of touch
whose name betrays
his birth: Epaphus,   40
born to a mother
touched by a god
in that fated hour.

Having spoken of him
in those rich fields
where my mother grazed,

now I recall
the tale of her pain.
What I will show,
though not expected,   50
will give men reason
as my story goes on
to trust my word.

If some passing stranger knows
the song of birds and hears my dirge,
he'll think the voice of Metis sings,
hawk-chased nightingale, Tereus' wife.

Kept from the river's verdant banks,
she sings a strange lament for her haunts:
composing the song of her child's death,   60
the child she killed with her own hand,
victim of a perverse mother's rage.

Like her, I weep in Greek fields
and tear my tender cheek,
tanned by the Nile's sun,
my heart unused to tears.
I gather the flowers of lament,
anxious to find a friend
in my flight from a land of mists.

But hear me, ancestral Gods,   70
favor our rightful cause!
If you truly detest pride
and don't provoke fate
by giving young girls away,
then marriage might be just.
A sacred altar protects
even fugitives from war.

May Zeus' will be done.
It's hard to trace his desires
for the ways of his mind reach out   80
through dark thickets, unseen.

He will land safe on his feet:
whatever his mind decides
must be done, is done.
Brilliant, it blazes out
even in the darkest night
and brings black fortune to Man.

And it hurls men to their ruin
from the high towers of hope,
but never by force of arms: 90
effortless, the work of a god.
Calm on his holy throne
he sits, yet works his will.

Let him look down now
on the pride of human stock,
how the stem buds again,
spurred by desire to wed,
blooming with evil thoughts
driven by the pricking goad,
the mind warped by delusion.   100

Of such sad things do I sing
my shrill, tearful lament.
Oh! Oh!
The dreariest dirge I sing,
I lament though still alive.
By the grace of the Apian hills
you know my foreign voice well;
again and again I tear
my soft Sidonian veil.

But where Death's away, and all's well,   110
these rites for the gods go awry.
Oh! Oh!
Troubles too hard to read,
where will this wave carry me?
By the grace of the Apian hills
you know my foreign voice well;
again and again I tear
my soft Sidonian veil.

The oars and the watertight ship
have brought us here unharmed,   120
helped by fair winds. I'm glad,
but may all-seeing Father Zeus
grant our wish in due time.
May a noble mother's seed
escape the beds of men—
ah no!—unmarried and untamed.

May the chaste daughter of Zeus,
on guard at her shrine's sacred door,
make her will match mine
and come with all her strength,   130
untamed, to save us, unharmed.
May a noble mother's seed
escape the beds of men—
ah no!—unmarried and untamed.

If not, we'll come with our boughs,
a dark and sunburnt race,
to Zeus, host of the dead:
if Olympians deny our prayers
we're ready to die by the noose.
The rage that pursues us, O Zeus,   140
as Io's seed, is divine.
Hera's jealousy rules the sky:
a fierce wind brings a storm.

And if it should happen like this,
won't Zeus be found guilty too,
he who disowns the child
he sired by a cow—his own son,
averting his eyes when we pray?
The rage that pursues us, O Zeus
as Io's seed, is divine.   150
Hera's jealousy rules the sky:
a fierce wind brings a storm.
(Danaus, father of the women, has entered as the chorus ends.)

DANAUS
Be wise, daughters, like your wise guide.
You came with me, a father to trust
and a leader at sea. Now, thinking ahead
to what may happen, here on this shore
I advise you to write these words on your mind.
I see a dust-cloud, voiceless herald
of an army (the axle-hubs aren't dumb),
and a crowd armed with shields and spears,   160
followed by horses and curved chariots.
Perhaps they are leaders, warned in advance
by messengers and come to see who we are.
But whether this band means no harm
or comes in anger, roused to a rage,
it's better to sit near this sacred mound
shared by the gods, for an altar's strength
is greater than a fortress, an unbreakable shield.
Come quickly now, and in your left hands
keep the white-wreathed suppliants' boughs,   170
emblems of Merciful Zeus. Speak words
suited to strangers: piteous laments,
needy words that newcomers use.
Tell of a flight, not caused by blood;
don't be forward when it's time to speak
or let boldness show in gentle eyes

and modest faces. Don't talk too fast,
but don't hang back: they'll take offense.
And remember, give way—you need their help;
arrogant tongues don't suit the weak.   180

DANAIDS

Wise words to the wise, father;
I'll take care to remember your advice to me.
May our ancestor, Zeus, look down on us here.

DANAUS

Yes, may he look with a gracious eye.
Waste no time but muster your strength.

DANAIDS

I should like to take my place beside you.
(The Danaids mount the stage.)
O Zeus, have mercy or else we're lost!

DANAUS

If he wills it, this must end well.
Now, invoke the bird of Zeus.

DANAIDS

We call on the sun's saving rays.   190

DANAUS

And holy Apollo, who fled from heaven.

DANAIDS

Having shared such a fate, he may pity men.

DANAUS

May he be kind to us, show us support.

DANAIDS

What other gods shall I invoke?

DANAUS

I see a trident, symbol of a god.

DANAIDS

He brought us safely, may he welcome us here.

DANAUS

The next is Hermes, according to Greek laws.

DANAIDS

Let him be the bearer of news that we're free!

DANAUS

Worship at the altar where all gods rule;
settle in this grove like a flock of doves   200
fearing the hawks, their fellow-birds,
related enemies, polluting kin.
How can a bird-eating bird be pure?
And how can one be pure who weds
the unwilling daughter of an unwilling sire?
Even in Hades after he's dead
he can't escape his outrageous acts.
There, they say, another Zeus
pronounces judgment among the dead.
This is the way you should look at things,   210
how you should answer to win this cause.
(Pelasgus, king of Argos, enters with his retinue.)

PELASGUS

Where have these barbarians come from,
dressed in fancy foreign robes
with bands on their heads? Not Argive, this dress,
nor from any part of Greece.
How did you dare to come unannounced,
no patrons to guide you, and not be afraid?
This makes me wonder. But I see branches

lying beside you before the gods
in the manner of suppliants: only this   220
would agree with a guess you were Greek.
For the rest, there's still a lot that's unsure
if you weren't here to answer yourselves.

DANAIDS

As for our clothing, what you said was not wrong;
but should I address you as a citizen of this town,
a temple warden, or the city's chief?

PELASGUS

You can answer and speak with confidence to me;
I am Pelasgus, son of Palaechthon.
I rule this land. The race of Pelasgians
who reap its fruits take their name   230
from me, their lord. My kingdom extends
through the land where the river Strymon flows
west toward the setting sun.
My borders extend to the Paeonians' land,
the place near Pindus, where Perrhaebians live
and Dodona's range, and then to the sea
whose shoreline cuts my kingdom short.
Within these limits I am lord.
This plain is named for a hero who healed:
Apis, the ancient doctor and seer,   240
son of Apollo, who came to this land
from Naupactus and purged it of a plague
of deadly, monstrous snakes that Earth,
poisoned by ancient bloodshed, had spawned.
Apis cut the curse away,
delivering our Argive land. As his fee
he's been named, since then, in our daily prayers.
Now you've heard the evidence I present,
tell us your race, but keep in mind
our city has no taste for long speeches.   250

DANAIDS

Our tale is brief. We are Argives by race,
offspring of a cow's divine calf.
The truth will emerge as our story proceeds.

PELASGUS

Strangers, your story is hard to believe.
How can this race of yours be Argive?
You look more like Libyans than the women here.
The Nile, too, might grow plants like these.
Such features are stamped on female forms
by Cyprian craftsmen. And in India I hear
there are nomad women who ride through the land   260
on saddled camels that move like horses,
close to where the Ethiopians live.
If you had bows we would surely have guessed
you were flesh-eating Amazons who hate all men.
But if I were told more, I might find out
how you can be Argive by birth and descent.

DANAIDS

There's a tale that once in this Argive land
Io was a priestess of Hera's temple.

PELASGUS

She was indeed, the story's well known.
And don't they say that Zeus slept with the girl?   270

DANAIDS

Yes, and these embraces were no secret to Hera.

PELASGUS

And how did the royal quarrel end?

DANAIDS

The Argive goddess turned the girl to a cow.

PELASGUS
    And did Zeus make love to the pretty-horned cow?

DANAIDS
    They say he turned himself into a bull.

PELASGUS
    So what did Zeus' strong wife do then?

DANAIDS
    She set an all-seeing guard on the cow.

PELASGUS
    What kind of all-seeing guard do you mean?

DANAIDS
    Argus, Earth's son, whom Hermes killed.

PELASGUS
    What else did she plan for the unhappy beast?   280

DANAIDS
    A fly that stings cows, goading them on.
    . . . .
    They call it Gadfly on the Nile's banks.

PELASGUS
    All this agrees with the tale I've heard.

DANAIDS
    And he drove her away on a tortuous course.

PELASGUS
    Is it true that she came to Canobus and Memphis?

DANAIDS
    Yes, Toucher Zeus begot a son with his hand.

PELASGUS

So who claims to be Zeus' calf by the cow?

DANAIDS

Epaphus, his trophy, rightly named.

PELASGUS

And he, Epaphus, did *he* have a child?

DANAIDS

Libya, who reaps the world's richest harvest.   290

PELASGUS

And what other children did she produce?

DANAIDS

My grandfather Belus, who had two sons.

PELASGUS

Then tell me the honored name of your father.

DANAIDS

It's Danaus, and his brother has fifty sons.

PELASGUS

Don't mince words; tell his name too.

DANAIDS

Aegyptus. Now you know my race;
pray give sanctuary to an Argive band.

PELASGUS

It's true, you seem to have an old share
in this land; but how did you come to leave
your father's home? By what bad luck?   300

DANAIDS

Lord of the Pelasgians, the misfortunes of men
change their color like a wing in flight,
never the same; who would have thought
this unplanned flight would scare native kin
to Argos escaping the marriage bed?

PELASGUS

Why do you speak in the name of these gods
as suppliants, with your white-wreathed boughs?

DANAIDS

So as not to become slaves to Aegyptus' sons.

PELASGUS

Do you speak from hatred, or of an unlawful act?

DANAIDS

What woman, if she loved him, would fault her lord?   310

PELASGUS

In marriage a woman suits her lord's needs

DANAIDS

But what man would force an unwilling spouse?

PELASGUS

Yet this is the way the men's power grows.

DANAIDS

And easy to dispose of miserable folk.

PELASGUS

So how should I do my duty to you?

DANAIDS

By not giving us back to Aegyptus' sons.

PELASGUS
 You drive a hard bargain; it will lead to war.

DANAIDS
 But remember, Justice protects her allies.

PELASGUS
 If she's on their side from the start.

DANAIDS
 Show respect for the ship of state with its wreaths.   320

PELASGUS
 I shudder at the shade of boughs on these shrines;
 the wrath of the Suppliants' Zeus is harsh.

DANAIDS
 Son of Palaechthon, Pelasgian Prince,
 hear me, Lord, with a willing heart.
 See me, your suppliant, flee like a calf,
 a heifer pursued by wolves to a crag,
 a place of refuge from where she lows
 to tell the herdsman of her distress.

PELASGUS
 I see in the shade of fresh-picked boughs
 a crowd of newcomers and the presiding gods.   330
 May no harm come from the strangers' cause,
 let no sudden strife erupt
 and catch our city unawares:
 we have no need of such things here.

DANAIDS
 May Suppliant Themis, daughter of Zeus,
 Lord of the Branches, look down on our flight
 and make sure it brings no harm to this place.
 But you, old in thought, learn from the young:

by sheltering suppliants you lose no respect;
the gods are grateful for the good man's gifts.   340

PELASGUS

You're not suppliants at my private hearth.
If some pollution threatens the city,
it's the task of the people to find a cure.
I'll make no promise till I've talked to *them*.

DANAIDS

You *are* the city, the people are you.
A leader's not judged: you rule your land,
its altar and hearth. You sit enthroned.
A nod of your head, a single scepter
determines all: beware of a curse!

PELASGUS

A curse is what I wish those I hate!   350
I can't protect you without causing harm,
but not to respect your prayers is unwise.
I'm at a loss and there's fear in my heart:
to act, not to act, to take a chance?

DANAIDS

Fix your eye on the watcher above,
the one who cares for those in distress
who sit beside neighbors but find no justice.
The anger of Suppliant Zeus looks down
and is not moved to pity by its victim's tears.

PELASGUS

If the sons of Aegyptus have rights over you   360
by your city's law, as next of kin,
who would be willing to contest their claim?
You see, you must plead this in your defense:
they have no such rights by your native laws.

DANAIDS

> May I never come under the rule of males,
> whatever happens! I'll chart a course
> by the stars to escape a marriage like that.
> Let Divine Justice be your guide
> and make a decision that respects the gods.

PELASGUS

> This decision's not easy. Don't make me judge.   370
> As I've said before, I won't act alone,
> although I am ruler. I'm afraid they'll say:
> "Honoring strangers, you ruined the city."

DANAIDS

> Zeus, who's kin to both these parties
> and weighs the lot of each, presides.
> He lays injustice in the bad man's scale,
> righteous acts on the side of the good.
> If these are weighed in fair proportion,
> why is it painful to you to be just?

PELASGUS

> We need deep counsel to bring salvation.   380
> The eye, when it plunges down to the depths,
> must be clear like a diver's, not dimmed by wine.
> So that this problem brings no harm
> to the state and turns out well for me,
> so that strife wins no prize and, by giving you up,
> seated as you are on the seats of the gods,
> we don't bring an unwelcome guest to our house,
> the ruthless Avenger, who even in Hades
> refuses to let the dead go free,
> isn't counsel needed to bring salvation?   390

DANAIDS

> Take counsel by all that's just,
> become our pious protector.

Don't betray the fugitive
driven here from far,
victim of godless attacks.

Don't see me snatched from the altars:
you who rule this land,
know the pride of men,
beware the wrath of gods.

Don't watch your suppliants dragged   400
unjustly from shrines of the gods,
seized by their linen headbands
like horses, their clothes torn.

Your choice affects your home:
an equal price to pay
however you decide.
Zeus makes justice prevail.

PELASGUS
    I've considered, and here it runs aground:
    I'm forced to make war against one side.
    The ship's timbers have already been nailed,   410
    though it still waits, held by the windlass—
    no course to steer that won't bring sorrow.
    A house's stolen wealth can be replaced
    by grace of the God of Property, Zeus,
    and when a tongue has missed its mark
    then words can charm speech back again,
    but to stop the shedding of kindred blood
    victims must fall to many gods:
    a great sacrifice is remedy for grief.
    Certainly, I withdraw from this dispute;   420
    I prefer to be ignorant than be expert in ills,
    but, against my judgment, may it turn out well.

DANAIDS
Now hear the end of my lengthy plea.

PELASGUS
I'm listening. Speak on; I won't miss a word.

DANAIDS
I have sashes and belts to fasten my clothes.

PELASGUS
These things are no doubt proper for women.

DANAIDS
I can make them into a fine device.

PELASGUS
Tell me what you're trying to say.

DANAIDS
If you won't support us with a promise we trust . . .

PELASGUS
What would this device of your belts achieve?   430

DANAIDS
To adorn these statues with a new kind of tablet.

PELASGUS
You speak in riddles. Speak in plain words.

DANAIDS
To hang myself from these gods right now.

PELASGUS
The words I've heard lash my heart.

DANAIDS

    You've understood. I made it clear.

PELASGUS

    True, these things are hard to grasp.
    A torrent of trouble comes against me;
    I have steered my course to a doomed sea,
    deep and uncharted, with no safe harbor.
    If I don't make good this debt to you,   440
    no arrow will outshoot the curse you describe.
    But if I stand firm under these walls
    and broach the issue of war with your kin,
    how can the tally not be bitter blood—
    men staining the ground for women's sake?
    Still, we must honor Suppliant Zeus' wrath,
    for he is the god whom mortals most fear.
    Come, old father of these girls, be quick:
    take boughs in your arms to place on the shrines
    of other gods, so the citizens will see   450
    signs you come as suppliants here
    before they blame me as they love to do.
    Then someone may feel pity at the sight
    and hate the hubris of this band of men.
    They'll look on you with kinder eye:
    all men are gracious toward the weak.

DANAUS

    It's worth a lot to have gained the support
    of one who's kind to strangers. But send
    some local folk as guards and guides
    so I may find my way in safety   460
    to the temple altars of your city's gods,
    for I'm not made by nature to look like you:
    the races differ by the Inachus and Nile.
    Take care that rashness breeds no fear:
    through ignorance, friend has killed friend before.

PELASGUS

> Fall to, men! The stranger is right.
> Lead him to the altars of the city's gods.
> Don't say too much to people you meet
> as you go with him to our sacred hearths.
> *(Exit Danaus with some of Pelasgus' attendants.)*

DANAIDS

> You've spoken to him, told him what to do,   470
> but what about me? What hope can I expect?

PELASGUS

> Leave your boughs here as a sign of distress.

DANAIDS

> I leave them here at your command.

PELASGUS

> Now step down into the temple grove.

DANAIDS

> But how can a public grove protect me?

PELASGUS

> We won't deliver you as prey to vultures.

DANAIDS

> But what if you give us to men worse than snakes?

PELASGUS

> Speak of good omens as I do to you.

DANAIDS

> It's no wonder our hearts fret in fear.

PELASGUS

> Too much fear undoes a prince.   480

DANAIDS
   Then cheer my heart with word and deed!

PELASGUS
   And so I will. You won't stay here long
   without your father. I myself
   will gather the people to make them all
   well-disposed. I'll instruct your father
   how to speak. So stay right here
   and pray our gods grant what you wish.
   I'll go myself to arrange these things.
   May Persuasion go with me and Fortune too.
(Exit Pelasgus with remaining attendants.)

DANAIDS
   Lord of lords, most blessed   490
   of the blessed, perfecter of power,
   mighty Zeus, hear me!
   Remove the pride of men
   justly detested; cast
   their black-benched boat of doom
   into the purple sea.

   Look on the women's side,
   on our ancient race sprung
   from a forebear dear to you
   and renew the tale of kindness.   500
   You who laid hands on Io,
   show you remember well!
   We claim our descent from Zeus
   through one who lived in this land.

   I turned to the ancient tracks
   to where my mother browsed,
   grazing on flowers in a field.

Found out, she fled, pursued
by the gadfly's maddening sting.
Io passed many tribes,   510
till, as fate decreed,
swimming the wave-tossed strait
she marked the bounds of Asia
and gave the Bosporus its name.
She tore through Asian lands,
past Phrygia's grazing sheep,
to the Mysian town of Teuthras
then sped through Cilician hills,
a land where Pamphylians live,
to the rivers that flow all year,   520
watering a fertile plain,
and on to Aphrodite's land:
Phoenicia, rich in corn.

Stung by the winged herdsman,
she gained the land of Zeus,
the fertile, snow-fed fields
swept by Typho's rage,
and so to the river Nile
whose waters bring no disease.
She was crazed with unearned pain,   530
tormented by the gadfly's sting,
a Maenad possessed by Hera.

And the people who lived there then
were shaken to the quick with fear,
blanching at the curious sight,
a puzzling hybrid creature
half woman and half a cow:
they marveled at the monstrous thing.
Then, who worked his charm
on wretched wandering Io,   540
maddened by the gadfly's sting?

He, whose rule never ends,
his power painless, his breath
divine. He stopped her flight.
So, as her tears fell,
she shed her sorrowful shame
and filled with precious freight
that rightly belongs to Zeus
she bore a blameless child,

whose life was long and rich.   550
So now the land exclaims:
This is Zeus' true son,
child of the giver of life.
Who else could have cured the disease
that Hera plotted but Zeus?
It's he who did this work,
and it's just as true to say
from Epaphus our race began.

On which god could I call
with juster claim than him?   560
Father who plants with his hand,
ancient crafter of our race.
Zeus who sends fair winds
is the cure for all our ills.

His throne is subject to none,
his strength no less than the strong.
He looks up to no gods in awe,
his act and his word speed
to effect the schemes of his mind.
(Enter Danaus.)

DANAUS

Take heart, children, things go well;   570
the people have voted, made their decrees.

DANAIDS

Greetings, father, dearest herald!
But tell us how the decision was made,
how the show of hands was won?

DANAUS

The vote was carried without dissent,
making my old heart young again.
The air bristled with raised right hands
that passed this law: "That we be free
to stay in their land, not subject to seizure,
inviolable. No man may take us away,   580
no local nor stranger. If force is used,
a local farmer who fails to help
will lose his rights, be exiled by decree."
This was put forward by the Pelasgian king,
who made a speech on our behalf
in which he warned of Zeus' wrath,
saying the city should never give it fuel,
how the twin defilement of citizen-guests
could not help but nourish harm.
Hearing such words the Argives didn't wait   590
for a herald's announcement, but raised their hands
to put these laws into effect. They heard
and eagerly obeyed the speaker's line;
the final seal was set by Zeus.

DANAIDS

Come, let's offer prayers,
call blessings on the Argives
repaying good with good.
May Zeus the Stranger watch
over honors from strangers' lips,
ensuring that they come true   600
and arrive at a blameless end.

And now it is time for you,
gods born of Zeus,
to listen as we pour out prayers:
may this Pelasgian land
never be burnt in fire
by the wanton god of war
whose cry is not for dancing,
Ares, who harvests men
in fields others have ploughed.   610
For they took pity on us
and cast a benign vote
respecting suppliants of Zeus,
a flock envied by none.
And they didn't vote for the males
dishonoring women's strife:
they had regard for the watcher
who exacts debts to Zeus,
he who can't be fought,
whose curse lies heavy on a house.   620
The Argives revered their kin,
suppliants of holy Zeus,
so with altars cleansed and pure
they'll win the grace of gods.

So let a prayer of honor
fly from our veiled lips:
may plague never empty this town
nor stain the soil of the land
with blood of Argive men.
Let the flower of youth not be culled,   630
and may Aphrodite's love,
Ares, slayer of men,
not shear its finest bloom.

Let the hearths where the elders come
blaze bright with wise old age.

So may the city be ruled
by men who worship Zeus,
God of Strangers, above all,
whose ancient laws rule fate.
May new guardians be born   640
ever to protect this land.
And may Artemis Hecate keep watch
over women giving birth.

Let no bloody slaughter
tear this city apart,
giving arms to Ares,
who brings no music or dance
but is only a father of tears:
the cry of civil war!
May the joyless swarm of ills   650
rest far from the people's heads;
let Apollo the Destroyer be kind
to all the youth of the town.

And may Zeus make fruits grow ripe,
bring crops in every season;
may their cattle have many calves,
may they thrive by the will of the gods.
May minstrels sing at the altars
songs that bring good omens,
let the lyre's friend, the voice,   660
rise from lips that are pure.

May the people who rule this city,
advising it wisely as one,
defend its honor well
and grant strangers their rights
before giving Ares arms.
May they honor their native gods,
bring laurels as their fathers did,

slay oxen in sacrifice.
For love of parents is third   670
of the laws great Justice wrote.

DANAUS

My dears, I approve of these prudent prayers;
now don't be afraid when you hear me speak,
telling you unexpected news.
From this look-out point where suppliants come
I see the ship—no detail escapes me:
the rigging of the sail, the screens on the side,
the prow with its painted eye on course,
its ear obedient to the rudder behind.
I can see the men on board quite plain: 680
their black limbs protrude from white clothes.
And the ships they command stand out well;
the leading ship is close to shore,
they've furled the sail, and the noise you hear
comes from banks of men at the oars.
Now you must face this calmly, with care.
Remember these gods, and I shall return
with men ready to defend your cause.
A herald may come to carry you off,
but nothing like that will happen, don't fear!   690
But if we are slow in bringing help
never forget your source of strength.
Take heart, my daughters. You'll see, in time,
the man who mocks the gods will pay.

DANAIDS

Father, I'm afraid. The ships are here,
rowed swiftly to shore. There's no time left.

I'm overcome with fear,
what did this long flight achieve?
Father, I'm out of my mind.

DANAUS

> The vote of the Argives carries full weight.   700
> They'll fight for you, children; I'm sure of that.

DANAIDS

> The dreadful race of Aegyptus is mad,
> and thirsty for war, as you well know.
>
> In their dark-eyed wooden ships
> they sailed with angry speed
> with their black-skinned host of men.

DANAUS

> But here they'll find a great number of men,
> their arms tempered by the noonday heat.

DANAIDS

> Don't leave me alone, father, please.
> A woman alone is useless, can't fight.   710
> Evil-minded and bent on deceit,
> their minds sullied, like crows
> not caring for altars at all.

DANAUS

> It would serve us well if they made foes
> not only of you but of the gods as well.

DANAIDS

> Fear of tridents and sacred things
> won't keep them from laying hands on us.
>
> They're arrogant with unclean rage,
> rabid and shameless as dogs,
> they pay the gods no heed.   720

DANAUS

> But they say wolves are stronger than dogs
> and papyrus can never master corn.

DANAIDS

> They behave like unholy slavering beasts;
> we must guard ourselves against their strength.

DANAUS

> It's slow business to rig out a navy,
> nor is it easy to anchor the ships
> or tie them safe with cables to shore.
> And even when the anchors hold firm
> the pilot feels nervous to put to shore
> on a harborless coast as the sun goes down,   730
> for night brings trouble, as wise pilots know.
> So the army will probably not disembark
> before the ships feel safely moored.
> And since you're afraid, look to the gods;
> they'll find no fault in an old envoy
> with a quick tongue—I'll soon bring help.

DANAIDS

> Oh earth, mountains, justly revered,
> what's to become of us? Where can we hide?
> In what dark corner of this Apian land?
> If I could become black smoke   740
> close to the clouds of Zeus,
> then I could fly up high
> and die unseen as dust.

> My heart is dark with fear.
> It quivers and I'm afraid
> of the things my father saw.
> Better to die by the noose
> than the hated touch of a man,
> better die before then
> and come under Hades' rule.   750

> How can I find a high perch
> where watery clouds turn to snow?

Or a crag too smooth for goats,
a lonely, overhung peak,
where vultures nest in rocks,
to witness my deadly dive
before I'm wed by force?

Then I won't object
to being prey for dogs,
a feast for the native birds;   760
the dead have no woes to lament.
Let death come, and arrive
before the wedding bed.
What other path is left
to rescue me from my fate?

Shriek your song to the skies,
a suppliant cry to the gods,
may it fulfill my wish!
Father, bring cure and peace;
don't look kindly on force,   770
respect your suppliants, be just,
omnipotent Lord of the earth.

The males of Aegyptus' race,
their arrogance hard to bear,
come running after me
with loud howls of lust:
they aim to take me by force.
But you hold the scales in your hands.
What is man's fate without you?
(Egyptian herald enters with attendants.)
    Ah! Aah! Here he is,   780
the attacker come from the sea!
May you die before you take me!

HERALD
    Come down at once from there!

DANAIDS

> I raise a cry of woe!
> Now I see the signs
> of the painful rape to come.
> Oh! Oh!
> Run to our safe haven!
> He revels in savage thoughts
> hateful to land and sea.   790
> Save us, lord of the land!

HERALD

> Hurry, hurry to the ship,
> fast as your feet will fly!
> Well then, with torn hair,
> branded with red-hot iron,
> or else with your heads cut off,
> in pools of blood—hurry up!
> Curse you, hurry to the ship!

DANAIDS

> I wish you had died on the great salt sea,
> you, your slave-owner's pride and your ship!   800

HERALD

> To the ship, I command you!
> Stop your resistance.
> Leave your seats
> near the city's gods
> and go to the ship.
> You have no rights
> in this pious place.

DANAIDS

> May you never again
> see the life-giving water
> that nourishes cattle   810
> and makes the land bloom.

HERALD

> I'm from noble stock
> and accustomed to lead.
> Soon you'll go to the ship
> willing or no,
> by force if we must,
> but you'll pay the price.

DANAIDS

> Aah! Ah!
> May you die in hopeless struggle,
> driven across the sea's domain   820
> by the east wind till you run aground
> on the sandy shoals of Sarpedon!
> *(The herald begins to mount the stage.)*

HERALD

> Howl, shriek, call on the gods!
> You won't jump out of Aegyptus' boat.
> You'll howl with sorrow worse than this.

DANAIDS

> Oooh! Ooh!
> You howl yourself like a dog
> come ashore, swollen with pride.
> May he who rules the Nile
> sweep your pride away!   830

HERALD

> Go to the ship, I order you now,
> as fast as you can. When I drag you off
> I'll have no respect for your long braids.

DANAIDS

> Father Zeus, your image brings ruin!
> He carries me off, step by step,

like a black spider, a horrid dream.
Aeiiiiiiii!
Mother Earth, Mother Earth,
turn away his terrible cries!
Father Zeus, son of Earth!   840

HERALD

I'm not afraid of these gods around here,
I've reached this age with no help from them.

DANAIDS

A two-legged snake is ready to strike,
a raging viper, what beast can I name?
Aeiiiii!
Mother Earth, Mother Earth
turn away his awful cries!
Father Zeus, son of Earth!

HERALD

Unless you obey me and go to the ship
I'll have no mercy for your pretty dress.   850

DANAIDS

Ah, leaders of the city, I'm overpowered!

HERALD

It seems I must drag you along by the hair,
since you pay no attention to what I say.

DANAIDS

We're lost, Lord! Unspeakable pain!

HERALD

Cheer up! Soon you'll see plenty of lords:
Aegyptus' sons, no dearth of rulers.
(Pelasgus enters with attendants.)

PELASGUS

You there, what are you doing here?
Why do you dishonor the Pelasgians' land?
Do you think you've come to a women's town?
Barbarian, you've gone too far against Greeks;   860
you've done much that's wrong, nothing right.

HERALD

What have I done that's so wrong and unjust?

PELASGUS

First, you don't know how to act as a guest.

HERALD

How not? I'm carrying off what I lost.

PELASGUS

To what patron here did you speak?

HERALD

To Hermes the Searcher, greatest of all.

PELASGUS

You spoke to the gods, but show no respect.

HERALD

I pay my respect to the gods of the Nile!

PELASGUS

But our gods are nothing, if I hear you right.

HERALD

I'll carry these girls off, if no one stops me.   870

PELASGUS

Touch them and you'll pay, sooner than you think!

HERALD

What an unkind way to speak to a stranger!

PELASGUS

I don't feel obliged to thieves of the gods.

HERALD

I'll go back and tell this to Aegyptus' sons.

PELASGUS

Your threat concerns those I care nothing about.

HERALD

But so I may know and make myself clear
(for a herald is bound to report each detail),
how and by whom shall I say this band
of their own cousins was taken from me?
When Ares judges a case like this   880
he hears no witness and takes no bribes.
Before it's resolved many men will fall,
their life gone with a final twitch.

PELASGUS

Why, may I ask, should I tell you my name?
In due time you and your crew will know.
As for the girls, you may carry them off
if pious arguments convince them to go
of their own free will, but this is the law
passed by the people's unanimous vote:
never to surrender these women by force.   890
This law's been fixed and bolted down,
not written on tablets or papyrus sheets
sealed with wax, but clearly spoken
by a free man's tongue. Now out of my sight!

HERALD

This means war's already declared.
May victory and glory go the men!

PELASGUS

Men are what you'll find in this land,
not folks who get drunk on barley-brew.
(Herald leaves with his attendants.)

PELASGUS

Now all of you, with your handmaids too,
take heart and go to our strong-walled city   900
protected by towers. You'll find many houses
built for the people—mine, too,
is no humble place. There you can live
with many others, or if you prefer
you may live alone. Choose what's best
and most to your liking. The choice is yours.
You're under my protection now
and the citizens who voted for this decree;
why wait for more powerful people than us?

DANAIDS

A thousand blessings for your goodness to us,   910
best of Pelasgians! But please be kind
and send our father Danaus here.
He's the one whose advice we trust.
It's for him to advise where we should stay.
And even if this city is well disposed,
everyone's apt to speak ill of strangers.
May all go well, here in this land,
and may the people speak no angry words.
(Exit Pelasgius with his attendants. The Danaids and their maidservants
descend into the orchestra.)

DANAIDS

    Dear handmaids, take your allotted places
    as Danaus decreed us each in our dowry.   920
(Enter Danaus with a bodyguard.)

DANAUS

    My children, we owe the Argives prayers,
    sacrifice, and libations like Olympian gods;
    without hesitation they've come to our rescue.
    Hearing my tale they showed kindness to kin
    but wrath to your cousins. To me they assigned
    a guard of spearsmen, an honored right,
    so I might not, by accident, meet my death
    and place an enduring burden on this land.
. . . .
    For these gifts we've received we must pay,
    from the depths of our hearts, with prayers.   930
    Beside the other wise words I've said
    to inscribe in your memory, write this, too:
    Time is what puts strangers to the test;
    and evil tongues are ready for use—
    it's easy to speak quick words of hate.
    So my advice is to bring me no shame,
    for your youthful prime will make heads turn.
    It's hard to protect summer's soft fruit;
    animals destroy it and so do men,
    birds with wings and beasts that walk.   940
    Aphrodite calls when fruits drip juice,
    and all who pass by lovely girls
    shoot seductive arrows from their eyes,
    smitten by desire. So let's not endure
    what we labored to avoid, ploughing the waves:
    bring no shame to us nor joy to foes.
    We have two offers of places to live,
    Pelasgus' and the city's, and both are free.

That much is easy, but keep my command:
respect discretion more than your life.   950

DANAIDS

For the rest, may the gods be on our side!
And as for our summer fruit, take heart,
for unless the gods have planned something new
our minds won't stray from their present course.

Come, let us sing together in praise
of the town's lords, the blessed gods
who protect the city, and those who live
near to Erasinus' ancient stream!
Enjoy our song, men of the guard;
praise shall govern this Pelasgian town.   960
Let's pay no homage in hymns to the Nile,

but to rivers that pour across this land
a gentle draught that bears rich fruit
and sweetens the earth with limpid streams.
May chaste Artemis take pity on us
and Aphrodite's rite come not by force,
for such a prize is tainted with death.

BODYGUARD

Yet we'll never neglect the goddess of love,
next, after Hera, in power to Zeus.
To the wily goddess all honor's due   970
for her sacred works. Beside her, Desire
and charming Persuasion, denied by none,
follow their mother; and Harmony too
has her special share of the goddess' work,
the whispers and smooth-worn paths of love.

But I fear that grief and bloody wars
lie ahead for the fugitive band.

Why else was it easy for those in pursuit
to sail here so fast? Fate will win out;
no one can surpass the will of Zeus   980
that is never crossed. May marriage come
as it has for so many women before.

DANAIDS

May Almighty Zeus keep me away
from marriage with men of Aegyptus' race.

BODYGUARD

Marriage would be the best solution.

DANAIDS

Those you would charm are not drawn in.

BODYGUARD

But you cannot know what will come next.

DANAIDS

How can we pierce the mind of Zeus,
plumb its depths and read what's there?

BODYGUARD

Then keep your prayers modest.   990

DANAIDS

Teach me what's best.

BODYGUARD

Don't ask the gods for more than your share.

DANAIDS

May Zeus, our Lord, avert
marriage we hate so much,
he who delivered Io

and held her with his healing hand,
turning force to kindness.

May he grant the women strength.
I'm content with the lesser evil,
happy if through my prayers   1000
right lies with the righteous
by the saving ways of God.

Prometheus Bound

Translated by
William Matthews

Translator's Preface

What did Prometheus do to incur such severe punishment? He was too good to humans, whom the other gods love to belittle as "creatures of a day," mortals, "mere May flies." Here's the whole story in a nutshell: whatsoever skills the humans have they got as a gift from Prometheus, as Prometheus himself tells us.

The gift of fire means that humans are no longer merely "daylight creatures," at night's mercy. But Prometheus gave more than that huge respite. Humans were "befuddled" and "witless," and "they had eyes but couldn't see, and ears but couldn't hear."

He taught humans numbers, "the most useful tool," and writing, "the mother of memory." They lived in caves, and Prometheus taught them to "build houses with bricks and facing the sun." He yoked beasts for them. His vaunting list of imparted lore and carefully taught skills goes on and on. In sum, he gave humans enough culture that, while the individuals of the species were mortal, the culture could be passed from one generation to the next. It didn't die, and thus the other gods couldn't feel toward it their easy, reflexive contempt. Prometheus narrowed the margin of perceived superiority between the gods and mortals, and some gods, Zeus foremost among them in both power and hatred, loathed him for that.

There's much sympathetic suffering in this play. Friendly visitors to Prometheus' crag characteristically assure him that they can feel his pain. And, according to the chorus,

> The waves of the sea let loose a cry
> as they break, and the deep oceans lament
> for you, and the dark abyss of Hades
> emits a groan, and the springs of the sacred
> rivers lament for your piteous suffering. (333–37)

Even Prometheus is moved by his own fate. "It eats at my heart to think of myself treated so badly" (338). Or, halfway through his list of the boons he made available to humans, "All these contrivances I gave to humans, and yet I cannot contrive to free myself from all this pain" (343).

He's powerless, he complains. Power is the play's nub. As ever, those who have it use it against others partly to prove they have it, and partly because they can.

But those who don't have power have speech (and, because of Prometheus, humans have the power to write speech down). And this play teems with boasters, taunters, whiners, monologists, phrasemakers, and filibusterers.

Here's Hephaestus speaking of Zeus: "one who wears power newly wears it harshly."

What cure did Prometheus offer humans for their fear of death? "I seated blind hope in their hearts."

When Io asks Prometheus who nailed him to the cliff, he replies, "Zeus by his will and Hephaestus by his hand."

Everyone's well spoken in this play, just as everyone in an opera sings well. It's the gap between eloquence and action, the slip between cup and lip, that defines tragedy here. Compared to the sleek epigrammatic shapeliness of the three quotations just above, the following rambling passage, in which Oceanus chides Prometheus, is slack and blobby.

> . . . But if you hurl such sharp-edged words
> soon Zeus will hear them, even from his far
> throne, and then your present pain will seem but
> a child's compared to whatever
> Zeus lays on next. Poor friend, give up your wrath
> and look to free yourself from trouble.
> What I say may seem old and usual
> advice, but you've brought pain on yourself
> by haughty talk . . . (229–37)

This sounds like a tapeloop message from the Polonius Inspirational Tape Company (www.arras.com?). It's a hallmark of a poet who wrote the phrase "blind hope" that his dullest characters emit ordinary wisdoms that are emotionally useful but rhetorically flabby, and that his shinier characters are quotable but morally reckless.

The play is full of characters explaining themselves and warning others. Relentless self-justification may well be natural to a play in which so much of the talk is frankly, compulsively about power.

The characters assume they're going to get or give a bad deal, and complain when they're on the wrong end of the transaction. Thus an eloquent bitterness becomes, for Prometheus, a moral posture. As the play draws near its shattering conclusion, Hermes chides Prometheus to give in.

> Unbend, you stubborn fool, unbend
> before you're staring ruin in the face. (788–89)

Prometheus begins his furious reply thus:

> You're wasting time in nagging me; you might
> as well try to educate the waves. (790–91)

He can't tell the difference between "It's not fair" and an elemental force. And what are his last words, as the play ends?

> . . . O holy
> mother mine, O sky that circles all and sheds
> its light on all, look on me now and see
> how I suffer, and how unjustly. (860–63)

Cast

POWER
HEPHAESTUS
PROMETHEUS
CHORUS OF THE DAUGHTERS OF OCEANUS
OCEANUS
IO, daughter of Inachus
HERMES, messenger of Zeus
NONSPEAKING
    Violence

(A crag in the Caucasus. Enter Power and Violence with Prometheus captive. Also, Hephaestus.)

POWER
    Here is the world's edge, the blank Scythian tract. No trace of
            anyone.
    And now, Hephaestus, you must fulfill the duty the Father
            saddled you with—to lash this criminal to the
            high crags with unbreakable shackles made of
            adamantine. For it was your very own ward, all-
            empowering fire, that he stole and gave to mere
            mortals. For such a crime the gods require
            punishment, and he must learn to honor Zeus
            and quell his love of humans.

HEPHAESTUS
    Power and Violence, you've done what Zeus required of you,
            and nothing holds you here. As for me, I've little
            heart for lashing a kindred god to this stark cliff
            in harshest winter. Yet I've got to find just such
            resolve, for he who slights the Father's com-
            mands cloaks himself with danger.

Wise son of Themis, giver of sound counsel, it's neither your will
nor mine that I fix you in unbreakable bronze
bonds far from all men here on this crag. You'll
hear no human voice, nor see a human shape.
The sun's fierce fire will singe your fair skin, and
you'll be glad each time night draws its starry
robe between the sun and you, but the sun will
be grimly back each dawn.
And this cycle shall be endless, for nobody yet born can free you
from it. This is what you get for loving humans
overmuch. A god like you should know to fear
the gods' wrath; instead you gave humans more
than their due.
Therefore you shall stand sentinel on this drear rock, sleepless,
your knee unbent. What moans you make will
bring you no relief, for Zeus' heart is hard: one
who wears power newly wears it harshly.

POWER

Tell me, why drag your feet and wear your pity? Don't you detest
a god hateful to gods because he gave their
privilege to humans?

HEPHAESTUS

He's my kin, and my friend, both. Is it so strange I feel these ties
to him?

POWER

Of course not. But do you refuse the Father's will? Have you no
fear of disappointing him?

HEPHAESTUS

You're steady in your heartless insolence.   10

POWER

Yes, I'll waste no pity on this fellow, nor energy on impossible
tasks.

HEPHAESTUS

Some possible tasks are hateful.

POWER

Why hate what you must do when you yourself have done
nothing to set the task before you?

HEPHAESTUS

All the same, I wish it were another's.

POWER

Every job chafes, except to be the lord of heaven, for only Zeus
is free.

HEPHAESTUS

I can't deny it, for this job chafes me.

POWER

Hurry up and chain him so the Father doesn't see you dawdling.

HEPHAESTUS

As you can see, here are his fetters.

POWER

Put them on his hands and swing that hammer. Nail him to the
rocks.

HEPHAESTUS

I'm doing it now. I'm doing my job.   20

POWER

Hammer harder. Don't stint with the wedge. Leave nothing
loose. We're dealing with an escape artist.

HEPHAESTUS

This arm, at least, can't be moved at all.

POWER

> Nail the other one as tight so that he learns, who thinks himself
> so clever, that's he's a dolt if he compares himself
> to Zeus.

HEPHAESTUS

> Only Prometheus could fault the job I've done.

POWER

> Now drive the wedge's obdurate edge straight through his chest,
> and hard.

HEPHAESTUS

> Oh, Prometheus, I moan for your pains.

POWER

> All this pity for the enemies of Zeus? You'd better save some for
> yourself.

HEPHAESTUS

> What you see hurts the eye to watch.

POWER

> I see this one getting just what he deserves. Encircle him with
> chains.

HEPHAESTUS

> I've got a job to do; you needn't nag me.   30

POWER

> I'll nag you and hound you as well. Now bend down and hoop
> his legs in tightly.

HEPHAESTUS

> There now, the job is done, and swift enough.

POWER

> Hammer those fetters with all your force, for he who judges our
> work here is severe.

HEPHAESTUS

You talk as lovely as you look.

POWER

Bah, Womanheart, don't blame me for my stubborn will and
        changeless mood.

HEPHAESTUS

Let's go, now his limbs are wholly harnessed in.
(Exit.)

POWER *(to Prometheus)*

Now what good is the insolence by which you stole a privilege
        from the gods and gave it to your May-fly
        humans? What scintilla of your suffering can
        they relieve? The gods were wrong to name you
        Forethought, unless they meant the forethought
        you'll now need to free yourself from this fix.
(Exit Power and Violence.)

PROMETHEUS

Bright sky and swift-winged winds,
waters of the rivers and teeming laughter of the ocean waves, and
        earth, mother of all,
and the all-seeing sun: I ask you to witness what I,   40
a god, suffer at the will of gods.
Through countless years I must wrestle,
though I am pinned here
at the will of the new Father of the Blessed.
O, O. I groan for my present misery
and for my misery to come,
and because I don't know how there might
ever come an end to my groaning.
What am I saying? I know my fate
and I have known it in advance;   50
no surprise is possible. I must wear my doom
as lightly as I can, for there's no changing fate.

I can't complain about it or stay silent.
Because I gave too much to humans
I've been pent in this rigid harness.
I sought out and hid in a fennel stalk
the secret source of fire, which humans used
as a teacher of all skills and a great
resource. This is the sin charged against me
and for which I stand here, nailed to account.   60
What's that? What invisible sound or scent
approaches me? Mortal, immortal or mixed?
Has someone come to the earth's edge to watch
me suffer, or for some other purpose?
Here can be seen a god in chains, enemy
of Zeus and all who enter Zeus' palace
hall, one who was far too kind to humans.
Now what? The nearby rustle of birds' wings?
The air whirs with the rustle of wings.
Whatever this means, I'm afraid of it.   70
(The Chorus of daughters of Oceanus enter on a winged car.)

CHORUS

    Don't fear us. Our friendly company
    has sped to your mountain by a rivalry
    of wings. No sooner had we gained our father's
    consent, it seemed, than the rapid winds urged
    us here. Deep in our cave we heard the sound
    of hammering, which drove off our usual
    modesty, and we set out unsandaled
    on our chariot of wings.

PROMETHEUS

    Alas, alas. Children of fecund Tethys
    and of Oceanus, who with his unsleeping   80
    current encircles the earth, look. See what chains
    bind me to my crag, a sullen sentinel.

CHORUS

    I see, Prometheus, and in my fear for you
    a mist of tears rose in my eyes to see
    you withering shamefully on your cliff
    in your adamantine bonds. New hands
    rule the heavens, and Zeus has forged new laws;
    what once was great he dwindles to nothing.

PROMETHEUS

    I wish he had hurled me beneath the earth,
    lower even than Hades, domain of the dead,   90
    and into limitless Tartarus, where,
    though he squeezed me into cruel chains,
    none would come to gloat and snicker at me.
    But I hang here, a toy to the winds
    and a sharp pleasure to my enemies.

CHORUS

    Who of the gods has so hard a heart
    that he exults in this? Who wouldn't share
    your pangs, except for Zeus? Stiffening rage
    has set in him. He keeps the breed sprung from
    Uranus captive, and will not relent   100
    until his cruel heart is slaked or someone
    pries his rule, so hard to capture, from him
    by some guileful strategy.

PROMETHEUS

    The day will come he'll need me, the very
    me he's tied and fettered; our Commander
    of the Blessed will need me to point out
    the plot against his throne and power.
    Not with honeyed charm shall he persuade me,
    nor with his fierce threats intimidate me
    to tell him what I know, unless he unchains   110
    me and compensates me for this pain.

CHORUS

>You're brave, and proudly resist bitter pain,
>and speak far too freely for your own good.
>It's left to me to fear your destiny
>and wonder what course you must sail to reach
>that kind harbor, the end of all your ills.
>For the son of Cronus is unswerving
>in his ways, and in his heart impervious.

PROMETHEUS

>I know how savage Zeus is, and how he
>keeps justice in his own hands. But one day   120
>his fierce mood will be mild when what I know
>has come to pass and broken him, and then
>what now is hard as oak will soften.
>And then he'll seek my friendship eagerly
>and my allegiance—one of these days.

CHORUS

>Tell us the story: on what charge has Zeus
>sentenced you to this shameful crag,
>unless, of course, the tale could harm you.

PROMETHEUS

>It hurts to tell the tale and hurts to suffer
>it in silence. Hurt lurks on either road.   130
>When first the gods were fueled by wrath,
>and gods wrangled against gods—some
>eager to supplant Cronus with Zeus (fools!)
>and others avid that Zeus not rule—
>I tried my best to advise the Titans,
>sons of Uranus and Earth, but I failed.
>Sly strategy they spurned, proud of their brute
>will and force, yes, arrogantly proud.
>But my mother (Themis, Earth—she is one
>but her names are many) had told me how   140

things were fated to turn out, and that
not by brute strength nor violence could
the cause be won, but by guile only.
And this I told the Titans, but they scorned
my advice. In the face of such disdain
my best plan seemed clear: along with my mother
I linked my fate to Zeus' ambition,
and he welcomed my support, and thanks in part
to my advice the vast gloom of Tartarus
seals in vanquished Cronus and his minions.   150
For all the help I gave the tyrant Zeus
this is the payment he has given me.
There is an illness deep in the core
of tyranny: the tyrant can't trust his friends.
But you have asked me why Zeus torments me;
this I will tell you. As soon as he climbed
his father's throne, he right away assigned
to the gods their privileges and gave them
their various powers; but to humans,
that unhappy race, he paid no heed, for   160
he planned to blot them out and install
another, new race to replace them.
Against this plan only I dared to stand.
I saved humans from utter destruction,
from swift, cruel passage to the house of death.
And therefore I am tortured on this rock,
to suffer pain and to be seen in pain.
I gave humans my first measure of pity
and now can win no pity for myself,
for pitiless is he who chains me here,   170
a spectacle that shames the fame of Zeus.

CHORUS

    Made of iron and rock would be the man, Prometheus, un-
        moved by your miseries. Myself, I'd rather not
        have seen them, and now that I have I'm pained
        throughout.

PROMETHEUS
>   My friends feel pity when they see me.

CHORUS
>   Is there not some further wrong that you did?

PROMETHEUS
>   Yes, I caused humans not to fear their deaths.

CHORUS
>   What cure did you offer for that fear?

PROMETHEUS
>   I seated blind hope in their hearts.

CHORUS
>   That was a great gift you gave them.

PROMETHEUS
>   Also, of course, I gave them fire.

CHORUS
>   These daylight creatures now have bright-faced fire?   180

PROMETHEUS
>   Yes, and from fire they will learn many skills.

CHORUS
>   These then are the charges on which Zeus . . .

PROMETHEUS
>   . . . tortures me with no respite from pain.

CHORUS
>   And is there no end in sight for your pain?

PROMETHEUS
>   Zeus binds me here at his whim.

CHORUS

> And when shall such whim change? What hope is there? Don't
>> you see what you've done wrong? I don't like to
>> say that you've done wrong, and you don't like
>> to hear it, so let's talk of it no more. Instead let's
>> seek a release for you from pain.

PROMETHEUS

> It's easy for him whose foot is free from harm
> to talk of right and wrong and to rebuke me.
> All along I've known what you just said.
> I knew it wrong and did it wrong and don't   190
> deny it. By helping humans I heaped
> trouble on myself, but I didn't
> foresee that I'd be punished like this, wasting away
> on this airy crag, this mountain top, alone.
> But, please, don't grieve for my present woes;
> go back to solid earth and find out
> what happens to me next so that you know
> a whole, completed story. Please, I beg you,
> join your fate to my troubled fate. Won't pain
> visit us all on pain's impartial rounds?   200

CHORUS

> Your prayer has sped itself, Prometheus,
> to willing ears, and so now with light foot
> I leave this rushing car and this thin air,
> the birds' highway, and head for solid ground.
> I long to know your story to its end.

(Enter Oceanus on a winged steed.)

OCEANUS

> I've come far, Prometheus, to see you,
> guiding my rapid mount without a bit
> and with only my will. I ache for you,
> you know that. No doubt kinship leads me,
> and, apart from blood, there's none I admire   210

more than you. Soon you'll know the truth of this
and know, too, I don't say such words lightly.
Tell me what I can do to help and you
will never say you had a better friend than I.

PROMETHEUS

What does this mean? Have you too come to gape
at the great spectacle of my torture?
Why have you come bravely to this land,
the Mother-of-Iron, from the stream that bears
your name and from the stone-roofed caves that you
yourself have carved? To stare at me and join   220
your pity to my pain? Now look at me,
a friend of Zeus, a willing accomplice
to his reign, and see what agonies
I am the home of, by his instruction.

OCEANUS

I see, Prometheus; and I have some
advice for you, smart as you are. You'll need
to know who you are, and then change yourself
to new ways; for the ruler of the gods
is new. But if you hurl such sharp-edged words
soon Zeus will hear them, even from his far   230
throne, and then your present pains will seem but
as a child's compared to whatever
Zeus lays on next. Poor friend, give up your wrath
and look to free yourself from trouble.
What I say may seem old and usual
advice, but you've brought pain on yourself
by haughty talk; you're not humble; you don't
yield to misfortune but resist it and
in so doing seem to call for still more.
Take my advice: stop your complaining,   240
since our harsh king rules alone and need not
consult anyone about what he does.
Now I will go see how I might help you.

Your job is to dam your stream of complaint.
You're smart enough to know how much a loose
tongue offers chances to constrain it.

PROMETHEUS

I envy you for being free of blame
although you dared share my troubles with me.
Now let them be no business of yours.
Talk as you might, Zeus will not hear you.   250
He can't be budged, and you could find
that coming here has put you in harm's way.

OCEANUS

You advise others better than yourself.
Outcomes and not opinions are what
matter in this case. Don't hold me back.
I'm confident he'll grant me the boon
I'll ask of him: to free you from these chains.

PROMETHEUS

I thank you and won't stop thanking you.
There's no more room in you for loyalty.
But don't trouble yourself, for it won't work   260
and won't help me—if you're of a mind
to trouble yourself. No, stay clear of this,
hands off. Just because I'm miserable
doesn't mean others need be miserable.
No, for I already lament the fate
of my brother Atlas, who in the West
shoulders the pillar of earth and heaven,
a load no one should lift. Pity shook me,
too, at the sight of Typhon, the earth-born
dweller in the Cilician caves, crushed   270
by force. Once he fought against all the gods,
hissing terribly from his fierce-clenched teeth,
forked lightning glaring from his eyes as he
strove to sack the very tyranny of Zeus;

but instead the unsleeping bolt of Zeus scathed
him, that down-rushing, fire-breathing bolt,
and seared away from him his vaunting boasts.
His heart was hit, his strength was burned to ash
and all that had been force in him was death.
Now he sprawls like a vast pile of waste   280
beside the strait that runs underneath Mount
Etna; high above him, then, Hephaestus sits
at his anvil hammering. Yet one day
rivers of hungry fire shall surge from there
and eat up Sicily, that vast orchard,
and char its smooth and fertile plains. A like
rage shall Typhon belch out, a fiery surf,
though Zeus' lightning left him but a cinder.
But you know all this: you don't need me
as a teacher. Keep your own needs in mind   290
while I drink to its dregs my sullen cup
until Zeus thinks to soften his his high wrath.

OCEANUS

Won't you think, Prometheus, how words can be balm to an
        unruly temper?

PROMETHEUS

Yes, if one can calm the heart in season and not try to lance it like
        a boil.

OCEANUS

What danger is there in my loyalty to you, do you think, and my
        daring?

PROMETHEUS

I see only a waste of effort and blithe, ineffectual good nature.

OCEANUS

Let me then have such a disease; a wise man could do worse than
        to seem a fool.

PROMETHEUS
  This fault will be seen to be mine.

OCEANUS
  Clearly your words urge me home again.

PROMETHEUS
  Take care: supporting me could earn you wrath.   300

OCEANUS
  His wrath, who sits so recent on his throne?

PROMETHEUS
  Be careful you don't rouse his wrathful heart.

OCEANUS
  Your fate will be my teacher.

PROMETHEUS
  Be gone then, go, and keep your goal in mind.

OCEANUS
  I'm all ears. See how my four-legged bird sweeps with his wings
          the birds' highway. He'll be glad at last to kneel
          and relax in his stable.
(Exit Oceanus.)

CHORUS
  I lament, Prometheus, your bitter fate,
  My eyes squeeze out a flood of tears
  and thereby irrigate my cheeks.
  This is a tyrant's work; dire Zeus
  has done this by his own laws only,   310
  showing how little haughty Zeus respects
  the gods of bygone days.

Now all the earth has cried aloud, lamenting:
all that was glorious in our great past
laments your fall, and laments your brothers' fall,
and all who live in sacred Asia lament
in sympathy for your great pain.

Dwellers in the land of Colchis,
the maidens fearless in battle,
and all who live in Scythia   320
around Lake Meotis,
at the very edge of the earth.

And the flower of Arabia bearing arms,
and the keepers of craggy fortresses
in the Caucasus, fierce warriors
bellowing for battle and brandishing
sharp-pointed spears.

Until now I have seen one and only god
in torture and unbreakable bondage,
and he was Atlas, the Titan,   330
the strongest of all, and now he groans
beneath the load of heaven and earth.

The waves of the sea let loose a cry
as they break, and the deep oceans lament
for you, and the dark abyss of Hades
emits a groan, and the springs of the sacred
rivers lament for your piteous suffering.

PROMETHEUS

Not for pride nor truculence am I silent. It eats at my heart to
       think of myself treated so badly. And yet who
       but I gave to humans what the gods keep to
       themselves?
No more of this; you know the whole story. But let me tell you
       how befuddled humans were before I aided
       them, how witless before I taught them to think

and to solve problems. I tell you this not to cast
blame on humans but to show how generous my
gift was.
For they had eyes but couldn't see, and ears but couldn't hear.
They stumbled the length of their lives through
a purposeless blur like the ragged shapes of
dreams. They did not know to build houses with
bricks and facing the sun, nor to work with
wood. They lived in sunless caves the way ants
live in the ground, and in such dark couldn't
tell winter from flowering spring or crop-rich
summer.   340
They worked without useful calculations, until I showed them
the risings and settings of stars, hard to discern
on their own. I taught them numbers, the most
useful tool, and writing, the mother of memory.
I yoked beasts for them, and made those beasts used to collar and
pack-saddle so that beasts might be substitutes
for humans at hard tasks; and I harnessed horses
to chariots and taught them to heed the rein—
horses, emblems of wealth and luxury.
And it was I and nobody else who gave humans ships, sail-
driven wagons that the sea buffets. All these
contrivances I gave to humans, yet I cannot
contrive to free myself from all this pain.

CHORUS

Your suffering is great. Your mind has gone wandering, and like a
bad doctor who has fallen ill, you've got no idea
what remedy to use to cure yourself.

PROMETHEUS

Hear more about the crafts and skills I gave to humans. The
greatest was this: when they fell ill, they had
no defense—no balm, no ointment, no elixir—
and lacking medicine, they wasted away, until I
showed them pharmacy so they could fend off
various diseases.

Also I taught them prophecy, and I first showed them which
dreams might come true, and I taught them how
to interpret ominous cries, otherwise so baffling.
I explained the omens of the highway and the
divination of the flights of crooked-taloned
birds—which augur well and which bode
poorly—their various habits, their mutual
enemies, their mating, their congregations.
I explained the smoothness of their entrails and what color in the
gall the gods like most, and what speckled beauty
in the liver. It was I who burned thighs wrapped
in fat, and the sleek shank bone, and taught
humans how to do the same. Also I taught them
to read signs in flames, so hard to discern.
Enough on these arts. What about the human treasure chest
beneath the ground—bronze, iron, silver, and
gold—will anyone claim to have discovered these
before I did? No one, I'm sure, who wants to tell
the truth. Here's the whole story in a nutshell:
whatsoever skills the humans have they got as
a gift from Prometheus.

CHORUS

So why lavish all your gifts on humans when you can't take
prudent care of yourself? Once you've shucked
off these bonds I think you'll be no less powerful
than overweening Zeus.

PROMETHEUS

Not yet. Not so. Destiny has a plan for me: I'm to be bent by ten
thousand agonies before I'm free from this pain.
Destiny overwhelms intelligence.   350

CHORUS

Who then is the helmsman of Destiny?

PROMETHEUS

The three Fates and the unforgetting Furies.

CHORUS

Is Zeus less powerful than they are?

PROMETHEUS

Yes, for even he bows to Destiny.

CHORUS

What awaits Zeus besides his present throne?

PROMETHEUS

You'll find out soon enough; don't ask me now.

CHORUS

This must be important, since you hide it.

PROMETHEUS

Think of something else, for it's the wrong time to talk of this. I'll
hide this at all cost; for only by keeping it will I
wrench free from my spiteful bondage and pain.

CHORUS

Never may Zeus, lord of everything,
oppose my will, nor may I dawdle   360
approaching the gods or sacrificing
beasts by the shores of the unceasing
Ocean, and may I not offend the gods
by what I say, and may these prayers
abide in my heart and never melt away.

How sweet it is to live long among
good cheer and hope, and to feed the spirit
with glad ceremony. But I shudder

to see you wracked by innumerable pains.
You failed to fear Zeus, Prometheus,   370
and you regarded humans too highly.

What have you got back for your gift, my friend?
What help can you expect from those who live
but a day? Didn't you see their frailty,
as weak as a dream, by which they are kept
in chains like blind prisoners? Never
shall they escape what Zeus has ordained.

This much I have learned looking on your pains,
Prometheus, ruinous pains. A dirge welled up
in me, so different from the song   380
I sang about your marriage bed and bath
to celebrate your winning Hesione
as your wife with your many gifts.
(Enter Io, horned like an ox.)

IO

What land is this? Who lives here? Who is it
I see nailed to these rocks in stark bondage?
What crime is this punishment for? Tell me
where it is that my wanderings have brought me.
O, O, O, here it is again, and again
it stings me, the gadfly, the ghost of earth-
born Argus. Keep it away, O earth!   390
I tremble when I see the shape of Argus
the herdsman with his ten thousand eyes.
He stalks me with his unearthly gaze,
for he's dead but the earth can't keep him,
and he's come from the dim underworld
to hunt me and drive me, starving,
along the sea-moistened sands.

The reed-woven pipe drones on and on
its sleep-inducing tones: O, O, O, just where

have my wanderings taken me? O son   400
of Cronus, what fault did you find in me,
what fault, that you would yoke me to misery
like this, that you would torture me
to madness, hounded by fear of the gadfly?
Burn me with fire or bury me in earth
or throw me to sea monsters for food;
but do not grudge me this prayer, O Lord.
I am at the end of my resources
and can't see how to end my suffering.
Do you hear the voice of the horned maiden?   410

PROMETHEUS

I hear the maiden's voice, the gadfly-haunted
daughter of Inachus. She kindled Zeus'
passion and now, hated by Hera, she is harried
endlessly, harried here and harried there.

IO

Why do you speak my father's name? Tell me,
who are you who knows to call me by name
and who knows the heaven-sent torture
that stings me and wastes me away, oh, oh.
So I come running, driven by Hera,
lashed on by torture and hunger, victim   420
of jealousy. Among all the company
of the wretched who has suffered as I have?
Tell me clearly what I still have to suffer,
what cure there is for my fate, what remedy.
Tell me, if you know, oh tell it to
the unlucky, wandering maiden.

PROMETHEUS

I shall tell clearly what you hope to know, not in riddles but in
                    plain speech such as friends speak to one
                    another. I am Prometheus, he who gave fire to
                    humans.

IO

> You who have done such good for humans, why are you being
> punished here?

PROMETHEUS

> I have just this minute finished the sad story of my calamities.

IO

> Will you then grant me a favor?   430

PROMETHEUS

> Tell me what favor you want, for from me you can learn
> everything.

IO

> Tell me who nailed you to this cliff.

PROMETHEUS

> Zeus by his will and Hephaestus by his hand.

IO

> For what crime is this the punishment?

PROMETHEUS

> It's enough that I've told you truth so far.

IO

> All right then, tell me how long I must endure these wretched
> wanderings.

PROMETHEUS

> It's better for you not to know than to know this.

IO

> I beg you, don't hide from me what I must suffer.

PROMETHEUS

It's not that I begrudge you this favor.

IO

Then why are you stalling?   440

PROMETHEUS

I'm afraid I may break your spirit.

IO

Let me be the one to worry about that.

PROMETHEUS

Since you insist, I'll tell you. Hear me.

CHORUS

No, not yet. Allow me, too, some part of the pleasure. Let us first
                hear the story of her suffering and let her tell us
                in her own words what brought her to this
                plight. Then you can tell her what travails are still
                to come to her.

PROMETHEUS

It's up to you, Io, to make these spirits happy, for not least
                among their qualifications is the fact that they're
                your father's sisters. It's well worth the effort to
                moan and lament for your harsh fate if you can
                win a tear from your listener.

IO

I don't know how I could refuse you.
I'll tell you clearly all that you would know.
Yet even as I speak I'm ashamed to think
of the storm Heaven unleashed on me,
and the marring of my beauty; I must grieve   450
when I think back on how this came about.

Night visions came repeatedly to me
in my chaste bedchamber, and cooed
to me, "Oh luck-kissed maiden, why are
you still a virgin who might get bedded
by the greatest? Zeus burns with lust for you
and is eager to meld with you in love;
don't spurn him. Go, child, to Lerna's meadow
with its deep grass where your father's flock grazes,
and let Zeus feast his ogling eyes on you."   460
Night after night these dreams came until at last
I took heart and told my father about them.
He sent many messengers to Pytho
and to Dodona to find what words
or deeds of his would most please the god,
but his messengers came back with murky,
twisted riddles from the oracles.
At last plain word came to Inachus
that he must exile me from home and country
and force me, footloose, to wander the world's   470
far margins; if he did not obey,
these oracles said, Zeus would loose on him
a flaming thunderbolt and blot him out
and his whole race. These oracles came from
Loxias, and Inachus obeyed them.
He threw me out and barred the door, with tears
streaming from us both. But Zeus could force him
to do this. And instantly I changed form,
and my mind changed, too. You can see my horns.
Stung by a sharp-toothed gadfly and leaping   480
as I ran, I sped alongside the river
Kerchneia, with its delicious water,
and past Lerna's spring. The earth-born herdsman
Argus followed me, ever angry,
and watched me with all his hundred eyes.
But then sudden death fell on him and I,
harried by the gadfly, that god-sent scourge,

was driven ever onward from one land
to the next, and that is my story.
If you can tell me what my fate holds next,   490
I beg you to do so, and don't cushion
hard news with lies, for there is no plague
worse than gentle words which are lies.

CHORUS

What weird doings! I never thought I'd hear
such a strange tale. Nor did I think that pain
so harsh to look upon and hear about
would prick my heart with its double-pointed blade.
Io, yours is an awful fate, and
I shudder to hear what has befallen you.

PROMETHEUS

You groan too soon and fear too soon. Wait until I tell you what
                        comes next.   500

CHORUS

Go ahead, tell all. For it is good for sufferers to know what they
                        must suffer next.

PROMETHEUS

The first thing you asked me you got easily:
you wished to hear from Io the story
of her sufferings. Now hear what remains
for her still to endure from Hera.
Listen, child of Inachus, and store
my words in your heart so that you may know
there's an end to your suffering.
From here, you'll first turn to the rising sun
and walk through lands no plow has furrowed;   510
then you will come to the Scythians,
nomads who live in wattled houses built
atop their wagons. They're warlike people

with far-reaching bows; keep your distance.
Walk instead along the surf-line
of the roaring sea, and cross their country.
On your left you'll find the ironworking
Chalybes. Beware of them: they're fierce
and suspicious of strangers. Then you will come
to Insolence, a river that deserves   520
its name. Don't cross it—it's hard to ford—
until you come to Caucasus itself,
highest of mountains, from whose craggy brow
the river issues. You must cross the peak,
neighbor to the stars, and then turn south
until you reach the man-hating Amazons.
One day they will live around Thermodon
in Themiscyra, where sailor-hating
Salmydessos rises rockily from the sea,
stepmother of ships. The Amazons will   530
gladly set you on your path: you will reach
the Cimmerian isthmus at the narrow gates
of the lake. Leave there with a good heart
and cross the channel of Meotis; ever
after there will be mention of your passage
and they shall name the place after you,
Cow's Ford—Bosporus. There leave Europe's
mainland and you'll be in Asia.
Don't you see now how the tyrant
of the gods is harsh in all things alike?   540
Leering Zeus sought to lie down in love
with mortal you and so brought down on you
the curse of wandering. This suitor
has filled your life with bitterness, maiden.
Yet what I've just told you is only
the beginning; there's much more to come.

IO

    O, O, O.

PROMETHEUS

> Are you weeping and lamenting now? What will you do when I
> tell what sufferings await you?

CHORUS

> Is there more of her suffering you will tell us about?

PROMETHEUS

> A stormy sea of agony and ruin.   550

IO

> What good is it then to live? Why don't I hurl myself off a cliff
> and crash to the earth and win at least an end to
> suffering? It would be better to die once than to
> suffer all my life.

PROMETHEUS

> You'd have a hard time with my fate, then, for I can't die. Death
> would deliver me, but there is no limit to my
> suffering until Zeus falls from power.

IO

> Can Zeus ever fall from power?

PROMETHEUS

> You would be happy to see that happen, I think.

IO

> Of course, for Zeus is my persecutor.

PROMETHEUS

> Then you should know that this will happen.

IO

> Who will wrest from him his scepter?

PROMETHEUS

He himself, with his witless plans.

IO

How will it happen? Oh tell me, if there is no harm in saying it.

PROMETHEUS

He shall make a marriage that will ruin him.   560

IO

With a god or a mortal? If it can be told, say which?

PROMETHEUS

Why ask with whom? This I cannot say.

IO

Is it his wife who will dethrone him?

PROMETHEUS

She shall bear him a son mightier than its father.

IO

He has no way to avoid this doom?

PROMETHEUS

None, unless it be me, freed from bondage.

IO

But who will free you, against Zeus' will?

PROMETHEUS

It will be one of your descendants.

IO

What, a child of mine shall set you free?

PROMETHEUS

Yes, in the thirteenth generation.   570

IO

This prophecy is more than I can understand.

PROMETHEUS

Then you shouldn't seek to know more about your sufferings.

IO

Don't offer me a favor and then withdraw it.

PROMETHEUS

I will tell you one or the other of two stories.

IO

What two? Let me know what my choice is.

PROMETHEUS

I will: you can know either what suffering remains for you or
        who will release me.

CHORUS

Grant her one wish and me the other, and don't let either
        story go untold. Tell her what remains of her
        wanderings and then tell us of the one who shall
        deliver you. That's what I want.

PROMETHEUS

Since you desire it so intensely, I'll
tell you both stories. First, Io, I'll tell you
of your sad wanderings, rich in lament;   580
inscribe the story on the tablets
of your memory. Once you cross the straits
that divide Europe from Asia, turn
to the rising sun and to the sun-burned

plains; cross the foaming sea until you reach
the flatlands of Kisthene, where the daughters
of Phorcys live, three ancient swan-shaped maids
with one common eye and a mutual tooth;
no place the sun shines on or moonbeams reach
contains their like. Nearby live their winged   590
sisters, the three snake-tressed Gorgons, who hate
humans. No mortal who looks on them lives
to tell about it. Beware these hags.
But hear of yet another fearful sight.
Watch out for Zeus' sharp-toothed hounds, who
do not bark, and the vultures, and the one-
eyed Arimaspians, skilled
riders of horses, who live near the spring,
flowing with gold, of Hades' river: don't
go near them. Then you shall come to a far   600
country of black men who live next to the spring
of the sun, where the river Ethiops is.
Follow its banks to the waterfall where
the Nile, from the Bybline hills, pours its sweet
waters. The river will lead you to
the triangular land of the Nile and there,
as fate has it, Io, you will found a home
for yourself and your descendants.
If any of this is unclear to you,
ask me again. I've got time on my hands.   610

CHORUS

If there's something left for you to tell her
of her dire wanderings, tell it. If not,
tell us the other story we asked for.

PROMETHEUS

She has now heard the end of her story;
so that she knows what I've told is no mere
caprice, I'll describe what she has endured

before she came here as a guarantee
of my account. I'll leave out the larger
part of the story and start at the very
end of your travels. When you had come   620
to the Molossian plains and the sheer
ridge that surrounds Dodona, where
the oracular seat of Zeus Thesprotian is,
the talking oaks, a marvel to behold,
you heard the oracles clearly describe
you as one who would soon be Zeus' bride—
does any of this sound familiar?
From there, harried by the gadfly, you rushed
along the shore to the great gulf of Rhea,
where fierce storms drove you backward on your path.   630
In times to come that inlet of the sea
shall be named Ionian to honor
you and your ceaseless wanderings. Take these
details, then, as tokens of my ability
to see more than only what is visible.
The rest I shall tell to you and her both,
returning to the part of the story where
I left off. There is a city, Canobus,
at the far edge of the world near the mouth
of the Nile: there Zeus shall make you sane   640
again with a touch of his unfearful hand.
You shall bear dark-skinned Epaphus, his name
recalling the benign touch of Zeus, and he
shall harvest the fruit of all the land
irrigated by the broad-flowing Nile.
Five generations after him, fifty
maidens will come to Argos, not
of their own free will but fleeing forced
marriages to their cousins. And these cousins,
their hearts engorged with lust, will pursue the maidens   650
like hawks harrowing doves, seeking an illegal
marriage. But the god shall begrudge these men

the women's bodies, and Pelasgian soil
shall be home to these brave women after they
slay the men in the dead of night. Each wife
shall rid her husband of his life, dyeing
a double-edged sword in his lustful blood—
thus may Love come upon my enemies!
But one among the maidens shall be
beguiled by love to spare her bedmate,   660
blunting her purpose; she will choose the name
Coward rather than Murderess, and she
shall in Argos bear a race of kings.
To tell this wholly needs a longer story,
but one born from her seed will excel
in archery, and he shall set me free.
This is the prophecy my mother,
the Titan Themis, told me. How it will
come true would take too long for me to tell
and what you'd learn from it would not help you.   670

IO

Eleleu, Eleleu! Pain and frenzy
are at me again, mind-twisting madness.
I'm stung by the gadfly's barb, a steel point
no fire has forged. My heart batters my ribs.
My eyeballs roll round and round. Madness
drives me on my course, and my ungoverned
tongue just babbles out a stream of murky
words to ride the billows of destruction.
(Exit Io.)

CHORUS

It was a wise man indeed who thought
this truth and then gave voice to it: it's best   680
to marry in one's own rank. May no one
who works with her hands long for marriage
to those puffed up by riches, or deemed great
because of the ancestry they come from.

Never will you see me, O mighty Fates, hoping
to share Zeus' lofty bed, or being wooed
by one who has to come to me from heaven.
I shudder to see Io's loveless virginity
ruined by her Hera-sped wanderings.
When a marriage has equal partners,   690
there's no cause for fear; and may the dread gaze
of no god fall on me with ruinous love.
There's no winning such battles, and they make
great misery; for what could you do
but escape Zeus and hugely displease him?

PROMETHEUS
Yet this prideful Zeus shall be humbled:
he plans a marriage that will cast him down
from his throne and power to oblivion.
And so at last Cronus' curse on his son,
which he spat out when driven from his throne,   700
shall come true. None among the gods but I
knows how this fate might be deflected,
I alone. So let him sit there on his throne
and fondle his thunder and turn in his
adoring hand his famous lightning bolt.
None of this pomp will fend off his sure end,
his ignominy and ample disgrace.
In fact he's even now preparing
his own irresistible opponent,
an enemy who will contrive a brighter   710
thunderbolt than Zeus', and a louder
thunderclap, and shatter Poseidon's
trident, scourge of the sea and the land.
And, as he topples, Zeus can think how far
apart are rule and abject slavery.

CHORUS
You'd be glad to see this god destroyed.

PROMETHEUS

Of course, but what I wish will also happen.

CHORUS

So we must expect someone to conquer Zeus?

PROMETHEUS

Yes, and he shall suffer more than I do now.

CHORUS

Have you no fear to speak such words?   720

PROMETHEUS

If I can't die, what should I fear?

CHORUS

Zeus could cause you far more pain than this.

PROMETHEUS

No doubt he will. I'm ready for it.

CHORUS

It's good to accept what Necessity decrees.

PROMETHEUS

Accept, worship, and flatter whomever
you like. But I begrudge Zeus everything.
Let him squat on his throne a few days more;
those days are few. But whom do we have here?
Zeus' minion, Zeus' step-and-fetch-it.
No doubt he's brought the latest news for us.   730
(Enter Hermes.)

HERMES

To you, the clever one, the paragon
of bitterness, you who sinned against the gods

and honored instead the creatures of a day,
you, the thief of fire—to you I speak.
The Father has commanded you to tell
what marriage of his it is you've been bragging
will bring him down from his throne of power—
and tell it straight, with no riddling. Don't cause
me another round trip, Prometheus;
you know full well that Zeus means business.   740

PROMETHEUS

Spoken with swagger and puffed up with pride,
as befits a lackey to the gods. You are young,
as is your rule, and you think that the tower
in which you live is a fort against sorrow.
Haven't I seen two tyrants cast from such heights?
I expect to live to see a third one
fall, more swiftly and more dishonored
even than the other two. Do you think I cower
before these upstart gods? Far from it.
Now scurry back the very way you came,   750
for there's nothing you will learn from me.

HERMES

You display now the selfsame pride
that brought you to this dreadful anchorage.

PROMETHEUS

I'd not trade my misfortune for
your slavery; be sure of that.

HERMES

Better to be a rock's slave, you say,
than to serve the mighty Father.

PROMETHEUS

Thus do the insolent show their insolence.

HERMES

> Maybe your punishment's not hard enough?

PROMETHEUS

> Not hard? I'd wish it on my enemies,   760
> and I count you as one of those.

HERMES

> So you blame me for your calamity?

PROMETHEUS

> In a word, I hate all the gods who took
> good from me and paid me back with pain.

HERMES

> Your words declare you more than slightly mad.

PROMETHEUS

> If mad means to hate one's enemies,
> well, then, I'm mad.

HERMES

> No one could bear you were you prosperous.

PROMETHEUS

> Alas!

HERMES

> Alas? Zeus knows no such word.   770

PROMETHEUS

> Time on its ceaseless path teaches all things.

HERMES

> But you still haven't learned discretion.

PROMETHEUS

Or I'd not be speaking to an underling.

HERMES

You will not grant the Father's wish?

PROMETHEUS

He who's been so very kind to me?

HERMES

Why, you mock me as if I were a child.

PROMETHEUS

And aren't you a child to think I'd tell you
anything? There's no torture nor device
Zeus could use to make me say what I know
until he loosens my cruel shackles.   780
So let him throw his proud lightning bolt
and confound the world with white-winged snow
and bellowing earthquakes: none of this will
bend me to tell him whose glad fate it will
be to drive him from his lofty throne.

HERMES

This plan may not be in your best interest.

PROMETHEUS

I've thought of that, and made my plans.

HERMES

Unbend, you stubborn fool, unbend,
before you're staring ruin in the face.

PROMETHEUS

You're wasting time in nagging me; you might   790
as well try to educate the waves.

Don't think I will turn womanish before
Zeus' vaunted might and change my mind.
Or beg him, with my hands upturned, to loose
me from these chains. I'm far, far from that.

HERMES

It seems to me I've said too much and got
for it no result. You're not softened,
and my entreaties don't dent your fierce will.
You're like a newly broken colt, the bit
clenched in its teeth, fighting the reins, bucking.   800
You're far too confident of your mere will,
which, by itself, uncounseled by wisdom,
is a sham strength, and really a weakness.
Consider what a storm of ruin, what
a wave of misery will break over you,
if you don't heed me. You'll have no escape.
First the Father will shatter this crag
with thunder and lightning bolt, and seal you
in the craggy innards wrapped in rocky
embrace; it will take long, dull work to reach   810
the light of day again. Then the winged hound
of Zeus, the bloody eagle, shall rend great
shreds of flesh from you, coming back each day
to eat some more: your liver shall be his meal
and his beak shall be black with your blood.
Look for no end to this pain until some god
volunteers to take your place and go down
to lightless Hades and the murky depths
of Tartarus. So this could be your fate.
I've spoken not boasts but the plain truth.   820
The mouth of Zeus does not know to lie,
and every word comes true. So think hard
what your fate shall be, and don't value
stubbornness above prudent advice.

CHORUS

    Hermes seems to us to speak with wisdom.
    He bids you not to be so obstinate
    and to consider wise counsel. It would
    be a shame for one so smart to choose ruin.

PROMETHEUS

    I knew what he would say even before
    he spoke it. There's no shame to suffering   830
    blows from an enemy you well detest.
    So let the lithe tendrils of fire come flying
    at me: let the air resound with thunderclaps
    and the fierce winds make all the world shudder.
    Let the earth be shaken at its root
    before the clamorous storm: let the sea's
    waves cross the stars' paths in a wild, surging
    torrent: let him lift high my body
    and cast it down into black Tartarus
    and the eddying waters of stern   840
    Necessity: but he'll never kill me.

HERMES

    This is a madman's plan, and his swirling
    words. How does your speech fall short of raving?
    And where did it fall short of sheer frenzy?
    You who sympathize with him, move back,
    get away from him, lest your wits be addled
    by the lightning and its deafening roar.

CHORUS

    This isn't what I want to hear: give me
    advice I can follow: these words of yours,
    for all their urgency, aren't right for us.   850
    You're asking us to act as cowards do.
    We'll bear along with him what he must bear,

for I have learned to detest traitors,
and there's nothing I despise like treachery.

HERMES

Remember that I warned you well and fully:
when you are caught by ruin don't blame Fate:
don't say that Zeus turned on you without
warning: do not do that, but blame yourselves:
for you know clearly the dire choice you've made.
Neither secretly nor all at once has   860
ruin wrapped you in its tightening net,
thrashing beyond all hope of rescue.

PROMETHEUS

Now it has changed from word to deed: the earth
rocks: in its depths the thunder sounds and sounds:
the burning tendrils of flame from lightning
bolts flash, and the whirling clouds swirl up dust:
all the winds' armies contend one against
the other: the sky and sea are mixed one
with the other: surely this is the global
storm Zeus has sent to torment me. O holy   870
mother mine, O sky that circles all and sheds
its light on all, look on me now and see
how I suffer, and how unjustly.

Pronouncing Glossary of Names

Stressed syllables are marked. The descriptions below are based primarily on the Oxford Classical Dictionary.

Achaeans (a-kee′-ans). Race of warlike bronze-age people who, with the Ionians, came into Greece from the north in the second millennium B.C. Homer uses the term to as a synonym for Greeks.

Acheron (ak′-er-on). River in Epirus that Homer assigned to the underworld because of the dead look of its waters.

Actor (ak′-tor). Companion of Heracles in his expedition against the Amazons; one of the defenders of Thebes.

Adrastus (a-dras′-tus). King of Argos, father of Deiphyle. One of the Seven against Thebes. The name means "the inescapable."

Aegiplanctus (eye-gi-plank′-tus). Mountain in the district of Megaris, southwest of Cithaeron.

Aegyptus (ee-gip′-tus). Son of Belus and Anchinoë, brother of Danaus. He gave his fifty sons to the fifty daughters of Danaus.

Aesculapius (es-ku-lap′-i-us). Son of Apollo by Coronis (or perhaps Larissa). Physician to the Argonauts, he was the inventor and, after his death, the god of medicine.

Agenor (a-jee′-nor). Phoenician king, brother of Belus, father of Europa, Cilix, and Cadmus.

Agbatana (ag-ba-ta′-na). The spelling Aeschylus and Herodotus used for Ecbatana, capital of the empire of the Medes founded by Deioces. The name in Persian was Hangmatana; the modern name is Hamadan. It was, like Susa, one of the royal residences of the Persian kings.

Alexander. Son of Philip of Macedon, conquerer of most of the known world.

Amazons (a′-ma-zons). Tribe of female warriors. The name, a-mazon, has been interpreted as meaning "without breasts," and they were said to cut off a breast to improve their aim as archers.

Amphiaraus (am-fee-ar'-ee-us). Son of Oecles, he was the seer who predicted the outcome of the expedition of the Seven against Thebes, but was nonetheless compelled to participate.

Amphion (am'-fee-on). Son of Zeus and Antiope; with his brother Zethus founder of Thebes.

Ananké (a-nan'-kee). Goddess of necessity.

Antigone (an-tig'-o-nee). Daughter of Oedipus and Jocasta, sister of Eteocles, Polynices, and Ismene.

Antiope (an-tye'-o-pee). First wife of Lycus, king of Thebes. Became pregnant by Zeus, tormented by Lycus' second wife Dirce, bore Amphion and Zethus on Mount Cithaeron.

Aphrodite (af-ro-dye'-te). Latin Venus. Goddess of love.

Apia (a-pee'-a). Ancient name of the Peloponnese, which it received from its king Apis.

Apis (a'-pis). Sacred bull worshipped in Memphis.

Apollo (a-pol'-low). God of music, healing, and prophecy. Son of Zeus and Leto, twin brother of Artemis.

Arachneus (a-rak-nee'-us). Hill in Argolis near Mycenae.

Arcadia (ar-kay'-dee-a). Province in the Peloponnese.

Areopagus (a-ree-oh-pay'-gus). "Hill of Ares" in Athens northwest of the Acropolis, and the council associated with it.

Ares (air'-ez). Latin Mars. God of war, son of Zeus and Hera.

Argos (ar'-gos). Strictly speaking, an ancient city, the capital of Argolis in the Peloponnese. But all the inhabitants of the Peloponnese, and even all the Greeks, are called Argives.

Argus (ar'-gus). Creature with a hundred eyes and so made an ideal watchman; appointed by Hera to guard Io so as to prevent Zeus from sleeping with her. Zeus sent Hermes to kill Argus, and Hera, unable to keep Zeus from Io, devised a new plan. She sent a gadfly to torment Io and keep her continually on the move.

Arimaspians (a-ri-mas'-pi-anz). Legendary one-eyed people who lived between the Issedones and the Hyperboreans in the extreme north.

Artaxerxes (ar-ta-zerk'-seez). Son and successor of Xerxes. Sometimes called Longimanus because one of his hands was longer than the other.

Artemis (ar'-te-mis). Virgin goddess of hunting, prophecy, and childbirth. Daughter of Zeus and Leto, elder twin sister of Apollo.

Astacus (ah-sta'-cus). Father of Melanippus.

Atalanta (a-ta-lan'-ta). Virgin huntress, companion of Artemis, mother of Parthenopaeus by Meleager. Promised to marry someone who could defeat her in a footrace.

Até (a'-tay). Personification of moral blindness, daughter of Strife and sister of Lawlessness. She presides over (and can be a designation for) the act of someone, often in a state of Hubris; what follows is Nemesis.

Athena (a-thee'-na). Latin Minerva. Goddess of wisdom and patroness of Athens. Daughter of Metis and Zeus, born from his head.

Athos (a'-thos). Mountain on the easternmost coast of Chalcis.

Atlas (at'-las). Titan, son of Iapetus and brother of Prometheus and Epimetheus. Traditionally held the world on his shoulders.

Atossa (a-tos'-a). Daughter of Cyrus who was married to Cambyses and then to Darius, by whom she had Xerxes.

Bacchus (bak'-us). God of wine and drinking, son of Zeus and Semele. The Bacchanalia were his festivals.

Belus (be'-lus). Ancient king of Babylon said to be the son of Osiris or Poseidon by Libya; father of Aegyptus and Danaus. His temple was plundered and demolished by Xerxes after the defeat of his expedition against the Greeks.

Boeotia (bee-oh'-sha). District in eastern Greece.

Bosporus (bos'-por-us). Narrow passage between Europe and Asia that connects the Black Sea with the Sea of Marmora. The name, meaning "cow's ford," is taken from Io, who passed across it in the form of a cow.

Bybline Hills. Mountains in Egypt where the Aethiop River had a waterfall.

Cadmus (kad'-mus). Son of Agenor and brother of Europa and Cilix. He established the country called Boeotia and founded the city of Thebes, which he populated with men (Spartoi) who sprang from the teeth of a dragon he had killed. He married Harmonia, and introduced the alphabet into Greece.

Calchas (kal'-kus). Soothsayer who accompanied the Greeks to Troy, and who told Agamemnon at Aulis that he must sacrifice his daughter Iphigenia.

Canobus (or Canopus). Egyptian city twelve miles from Alexandria.

Capaneus (ka-pa-nay'-us). One of the Seven against Thebes. As he climed the walls of Thebes he boasted that he would take the city even without the help of Zeus, and was thereupon struck by lightning.

Caucasus (kaw'-ka-sus). Mountain range that runs from the Black Sea to the Caspian Sea.

Chalcis. (kal'-kis). City in Euboea.

Chalybes (ka'-li-beez). People of Asia Minor near the Pontus who attacked the Persians in their retreat.

Chios (kee'-os). Now Scio, island in the Aegean Sea between Lesbos and Samos.

Cilicia (si-li'-si-a). Country in Asia Minor west of the Euphrates, named for Cilix, son of Agenor.

Cimmeria (sim-meer'-i-a). Nation on the western coast of Italy. The Cimmerians were said to live in caves, shunning the sunlight, and some writers placed the Styx, the Phlegethon, and all the rivers of Hades in this region.

Cithaeron (ki-thye'-ron). Mountain in Boeotia sacred to Zeus and the Muses.

Cocytus (ko-kee'-tus). River in Epirus, thought to be one of the rivers of Hades.

Colchis (kol'-kis). Country in Asia east of the Black Sea and north of Armenia; the birthplace of Medea.

Corinth (kor'-inth). City in Greece on the Isthmus of Corinth.

Creon (kray'-on). Brother of Jocasta and king of Thebes after the death of Polynices and Eteocles. Father of Megareus.

Cronus (kro'-nus). Latin Saturn. Titan, son of Heaven (Uranus) and Earth (Gaia). He married his sister Rhea; their children included the gods and goddesses Hestia, Demeter, Hera, Hades, Poseidon, and Zeus, who overthrew him.

Cyprus (Greek keep'-rus or koop'-rus). Large Mediterranean island where Aphrodite was born. She was the chief diety of the place and is therefore sometimes called Cypris.

Danaus (da-nah'-us). Son of Belus and Anchinoë and co-ruler of Egypt with his brother Aegyptus. Father of the fifty Danaids, all of whom except Hypermestra killed their husbands, the sons of Aegyptus.

Darius (da-rye'-us). King of Persia and father of Xerxes by Atossa.

Daryavaush (dar-ya-vaush'). Darius' name in Persian.

Deiphyle (dey'-i-fyl) Daughter of Adrastus, wife of Tydeus.

Delos (del'-os). Island north of Naxos (one of the Cyclades), said at one time to be floating, where Leto gave birth to Apollo and Artemis.

Delphi (del'-fye). Town on the southwest side of Mount Parnassus where the Pythia gave oracular messages inspired by Apollo.

Delphus (del'-fus). Son of Apollo who built Delphi and consecrated it to his father.

Dionysus (di-o-nee'-sus). Another name for Bacchus. The Dionysia was the wine festival in the god's honor.

Dirce (dir'-see). Second wife of Lycus, king of Thebes. He married her after divorcing Antiope. After the divorce, Antiope became pregnant by Zeus, and Dirce, suspecting Lycus was the father, imprisoned and tormented Antiope, who nonetheless escaped and bore Amphion and Zethus on Mount Cithaeron. When they murdered Dirce, she was turned into a spring near Thebes.

Dodona (do-doh'-na). Sanctuary of Zeus in Thesprotia in Epirus. It had a grove of oak trees that were sacred to the god.

Engia (en-gee'-a). Gulf of the Aegean Sea near Sunium.

Epaphus (e-pah'-fus). Son of Zeus and Io, founder of Memphis in Egypt. Father of Libya.

Epirus (ep-aye'-rus). Area of northwest Greece.

Erasinus (er-a-see'-nus). River in the Peloponnese in Argos.

Eretria (e-re-tree'-a). City in Euboea.

Erinyes (er-in'-ees) (singular Erinys). The Furies, the spirits of divine vengeance, who later became the Eumenides.

Eteocles (e-tee'-o-cleez). Son of Oedipus and Jocasta, brother of Polynices, Antigone, and Ismene.

Eteoclus (e-tee-oh'-clus). Son of Iphis, one of the Seven against Thebes.

Etna (et'-na). Volcano in Sicily.

Euboea (you-bee'-a). Long island that stretches from the Gulf of Pagasae to Andros. Its chief cities were Chalcis and Eretria.

Eumenides (you-men'-i-des). The name for the Erinyes in their benevolent aspect.

Euripus (you-rip'-us). Strait that separates the island of Euboea from the coast of Boeotia.

Europa (yoo-roh′-pa). Daughter of Agenor. Carried off by Zeus in the form of a bull, mother by him of Minos and Sarpedon.

Furies. See Erinyes and Eumenides.

Gaia (gay′-a). Ancient personification of the earth.

Gorgons (gor′-gonz). Daughers of Phorcys. Three monstrous sisters with golden wings and hair entwined with serpents. Medusa, the only mortal one, is best known.

Hades (hay′-dez). Latin Pluto. God of the underworld (so the name is used for the underworld itself). Son of the Titans Cronus and Rhea, brother of Demeter, Hades, Hera, Hestia, Poseidon, and Zeus. Husband of Persephone.

Hecate (he′-ka-te or hek′-at). Goddess who presided over magic and witchcraft. Often conflated with Persephone and Artemis.

Hellas (hel′-as). Name originally applied to a territory and a small tribe in southern Thessaly, it later came to include all Greeks.

Hephaestus (hef-fes′-tus). Latin Vulcan. God of fire and smithing.

Hera (her′-a). Latin Juno. Wife and sister of Zeus, and queen of heaven.

Heracles (her′-a-kleez). Latin Hercules. Son of Zeus by Alcmena. He was tormented by Hera and made to perform many arduous labors.

Hermes (her′-mes). Latin Mercury. Son of Zeus and the nymph Maia. He was the messenger god and patron of messengers and merchants.

Hesione (hes-eye′-o-nee). Oceanid, wife of Prometheus.

Hippomedon (hip-pom′-e-don). Son of Misimachus and Mythidice, one of the Seven against Thebes.

Hyperbius. Son of Oenops, one of the defenders of Thebes.

Hypermestra (hy-per-mes′-tra). Daugher of Danaus, wife of Lynceus, the only Danaid who did not kill her husband.

Iapetus (i-ap′-e-tus). Titan, son of Gaia and Uranus, father of Prometheus, Epimetheus, and Atlas.

Ida (eye′-da). Mountain near Troy; more properly the whole ridge of mountains that are the source of the Simois, Scamander, Aesepus, and other rivers.

Inachus (in′-ak-us). Founder of Argos, father of Io.

Io (eye′-o). Daughter of Inachus. Loved by Zeus and turned by him into a white cow to conceal his adultery from Hera. Mother of Epaphus.

Ismene (iz-may'-nay). Daughter of Jocasta and Oedipus, sister of Antigone, Polynices, and Eteocles.

Ismenus (iz-may'-nus). River near Thebes.

Jocasta (jo-cas'-ta). Mother and wife of Oedipus, daughter of Menoeceus, sister of Creon.

Kerchneia (kerk-nye'-a). Lake in Argolis.

Khshayarsha (sha-yar'-sha). Xerxes' name in Persian.

Kissa (kis'-a). River that flows into the Pontus.

Kisthene (kis-thee'-nee). Plain where the Gorgons lived.

Knidos (nee'-dos). Town and promontory in Caria.

Laius (lay'-us). Father of Oedipus.

Lasthenes (las-thee'-neez). One of the defenders of Thebes.

Lemnos (lem'-nos). Island in the Aegean Sea sacred to Hephaestus, now called Stalimine.

Lerna (ler'-na). Lake in the Peloponnese where the Hydra lived.

Lesbos (les'-bos). Large island in the Aegean Sea just off the Turkish coast, now called Mitilini.

Leto (lee'-to). Latin Latona. Titaness, daughter of Coeus and Phoebe, loved by Zeus to whom she bore Apollo and Artemis.

Libya (lib'-ya). General name for North Africa, taken from the name of the daughter of Epaphus and Cassiopia who bore Agenor and Belus to Poseidon.

Loxias (lok'-see-us). Name for Apollo

Lynceus (lin-kee'-us). Son of Aegyptus who married Hypermestra, one of the daughters of Danaus. She spared his life.

Lyrceia (lir-kye'-a). City near Argos to which Lynceus fled when Hypermestra spared his life.

Macedon. The part of Greece north of the Strymon River.

Maenads (mee'-nads). The Bacchantes.

Maeotis (may-oh'-tis). Large lake or part of the sea between Europe and Asia at the north of the Black Sea, now called the Sea of Azov. The Amazons lived on its shores.

Maia (mye'-a). One of the Pleiades, mother of Hermes by Zeus.

Marathon. Village in Attica where 10,000 Athenians and 1000 Plataeans under the command of Mitiades defeated the Persian army of 100,000 infantry and 10,000 cavalry on September 28, 490 B.C. According to Herodotus, the Athenians lost 192 men and the Persians 6300.

Medus (mee'-dus). Son of Medea by Aegeus, king of Athens.

Megara (me-gar'-a). City in Achaea halfway between Athens and Corinth. It was named after Megareus the son of Poseidon or Megareus the son of Apollo, and has nothing to do with Creon's son of that name.

Megareus (me-gar'-ee-us). Son of Creon, one of the defenders of Thebes.

Melanippus (mel-an-ip'-us). Theban general, son of Astacus.

Meleager (mel-ee-ay'-ger). Son of Oeneus king of Aetolia (or of Ares) and Althaea. Fell in love with Atalanta, by whom he had Parthenopaeus.

Memphis (mem'-fis). City in Egypt founded by Epaphus.

Merope (mer'-o-pay). Wife of king Polybus of Corinth and foster mother to Oedipus.

Minos (mye'-nus). King of Crete, son of Zeus and Europa.

Molossia (mo-los'-i-a). The part of Epirus in which the city of Thesprotia was located. It was ruled by Molossus and was famous for its dogs.

Molossus (mo-los'-us). Son of Neoptolemus and Andromache.

Mycenae (my-se'-nee). Town in the Peloponnese where Agamemnon ruled.

Mysia (miz'-i-a). Country in Asia Minor.

Naupactus (now-pak'-tus). City in Aetolia, now called Lepanto.

Necessity. See Ananké

Nisus (nis'-us). King of Megara, whose fate depended on his maintaining a lock of purple hair. When his daughter Scylla fell in love with Minos who had laid siege to Megara, she cut off this lock of hair from her father's head, and the town immediately fell.

Oceanus (o-see'-a-nus). God of the sea, son of Uranus and Gaia, father of the Oceanids and river gods.

Oecles (ee'-kleez). Father of Amphiaraus.

Oedipus (ed'-i-pus). Son of Laius and Jocasta; husband of Jocasta, father of Antigone, Ismene, Polynices, and Eteocles.

Oenops (ee'-nops). Father of Hyperbius.

Olympus (o-lim'-pus). Mountain of Thessaly so tall that the Greeks believed it touched the heavens; it was therefore the home of the Olympian gods.

Onca (on'-ka). Name for Athena as a goddess of death. The name means "pear tree"; the blossom has white petals and white is frequently a funereal color. Athena had a grove of sacred pear trees in Boeotia.

Paeonia (pee-oh'-nee-a). country of Macedonia named after Paeon, a son of Endymion.

Palaechthon (pal-ike'-thon). Father of Pelasgus.

Pallas (pal'-us). Name for Athena.

Pamphylia (pam-phil'-i-a). Area in the southern coastal plain of Turkey.

Parnassus (par-nas'-us). Mountain near Delphi, home of the Muses.

Parthenopaeus (par-then-o-pye'-us). Son of Meleager and Atalanta, one of the Seven against Thebes.

Pelasgus (pel-as'-us). Son of Palaechthon, ruler in Sicyon who gave his name to the ancient inhabitants of the Peloponnese.

Peloponnese (pel-o-po-neez'). The large peninsula of the southern part of mainland Greece.

Perrhaebia (per-hye'-bee-a). Part of Thessaly along the banks of the Peneus River.

Persephone (per-sef'-o-nee). Latin Proserpine. Daughter of Demeter, abducted by Hades who made her his queen. She spends six months a year in the underworld and six in the world of light.

Phocis (foh'-kiss). District of Greece next to Boeotia on the Gulf of Corinth.

Phoebe (fee'-bee). Name given to Artemis as the moon goddess.

Phoebus (fee'-bus). Name for Apollo.

Phorcys (for'-kis). Sea god who was the father of the Gorgons.

Phrygia (fri'-jee-a). Country in Asia Minor in which Cybele was worshipped and Troy was the most prominent city.

Pindus (pin'-dus). Mountain or chain of mountains between Thessaly, Macedonia, and Epirus.

Polybus (pol'-i-bus). King of Corinth. He and his wife Merope, childless, adopted the infant Odysseus.

Polynices (po-lee-nye'-seez). Son of Oedipus and Jocasta, brother of Eteocles, Antigone, and Ismene.

Polyphontes (pol-i-fon'-teez). Theban general under Eteocles. The name means "killer of many."

Poseidon (po-sye'-don). Latin Neptune. God of the sea, son of the titans

Cronus and Rhea, brother of Demeter, Hades, Hera, Hestia, and Zeus.

Procne (prok.-nee). Wife of Tereus, mother of Itys, sister of Philomela. Itys was changed into a pheasant, his mother into a swallow, and his father into an owl.

Prometheus (pro-mee'-the-us). Son of the Titan Iapetus and the Oceanid Clymene, brother of Atlas, Menoetius, and Epimetheus. He stole fire from the chariot of the sun and brought it down to earth on a fennel stalk, for which crime he was tied to a rock for 30,000 years with a vulture feeding on his liver. Eventually rescued by Heracles.

Psyttaleia (sit-a-lay'-a). Small island in the strait near Salamis.

Pytho (pye'-tho). Ancient name of Delphi, called that because of the great serpent Apollo killed there.

Rhea (ree'-a). Titaness, wife of Cronus and mother of Zeus and his brothers and sisters.

Salamis (sal'-a-mis). Island in the Saronic Gulf opposite Eleusis, now called Kolouri. Famous for the battle of October 20, 480 B.C. in which the Greek fleet of 280 ships defeated the Persian fleet of more than 2000 ships.

Salmydessos (sal-mee-des'-sos). Bay in the Black Sea.

Samos (sam'-os). Island in the Aegean Sea off the coast of Asia Minor. The Samians assisted the Greeks against Xerxes.

Sardis (sar'-dis). Now called Sart, town in Asia Minor at the foot of Mount Tmolus that was the capital of the Lydians.

Saronic Gulf. The indentation of the sea opposite the Gulf of Corinth, with the Isthmus of Corinth between them.

Sarpedon (sar-pee'-don). Son of Zeus and Europa. He tried to displace Minos as king of Crete but failed. He left Crete to found the town of Miletus and joined the Trojans against the Greeks.

Scamander (ska-man'-der). River near Troy.

Scylla (sil'-a, Greek skil'-a). Daughter of Nisus whom she betrayed for the love of Minos, king of Crete. When the latter spurned her, she threw herself into the sea and was transformed to rocks dangerous to sailors.

Scythia (skith'-i-a). Area north and northeast of the Black Sea.

Sidon (sye'-don). Town in Syria on the Mediterranean coast.

Sphinx. Monster with the head and breasts of a woman, the body of a dog, the tail of a snake, the wings of a bird, the paws of a lion, and a human voice. Hera sent her to Boeotia, where she proposed riddles to the inhabitants and devoured those who failed to answer correctly. When Oedipus gave the correct answer, she destroyed herself.

Strymon (stry'-mon). River that is the border between Thrace and Macedon.

Susa (soo'-sa). Darius' capital city.

Tartarus (tar'-ta-rus). One of the regions of Hades where the guiltiest were punished.

Tethys (teth'-is). Sea goddess, daughter of Uranus and Gaia and wife of Oceanus.

Teuthras (tooth'-ras). Mysian king who adoped Auge after she had been raped by Heracles and delivered a son, Telephus.

Thebes (Theebz). City in Boeotia.

Themis (them'-is). Daughter of Uranus and Gaia who married Zeus and was the mother of the Horae (the Hours)—Diké (justice), Eirene (peace), Eunomia (good order)—and the Moirae (the Fates).

Themiscyra (them-is-kye'-ra). Amazonian town in Cappadocia at the mouth of the Thermodon.

Thermodon (ther'-mo-don). River in Cappadocia that flows into the Black Sea.

Thesprotia (thes-pro'-ti-a). Part of Epirus where the Acheron and Cocytus rivers flowed and where Zeus' shrine at Dodona was located.

Thessaly (thes'-a-lee). Territory to the north of Greece proper.

Thrace (Thrays). Country south of Scythia and west of Macedon, area encompassing most of the world north of the Black Sea.

Titans. Legendary predecessors of the Olympian gods.

Tmolus (tmol'-us). King of Lydia who raped a nymph at the foot of Artemis' altar. For this impiety he was killed by a bull. The mountain where he was buried was named after him.

Triton (try'-ton). Fish-tailed sea-creature, often portrayed as blowing a conch.

Tydeus (tid'-ee-us). Son of Oeneus, king of Calydon, married Deiphyle, daughter of Adrastus, king of Argos, who was also father-in-law of Polynices. One of the Seven against Thebes.

Typhon (tye'-fon). Hundred-headed giant who made war against the gods and was crushed under Mount Etna.

Uranus (you'-ra-nus, Greek our'-an-us). Ancient personification of the sky, produced by and then consort of Gaia, overcome by his son Cronus.

Xerxes (zerk'-seez). Son of Darius, king of Persia who led the expedition against Greece

Zeus (zoos). Latin Jupiter. Son of the Titans Cronus and Rhea, brother of Hestia, Demeter, Hera (whom he married), Hades, and Poseidon. After he overthrew Cronus he became the chief Greek god.

About the Translators

GAIL HOLST-WARHAFT graduated from Melbourne University and received her Ph.D. in comparative literature from Cornell University, where she now teaches classics and modern Greek and is active in Balkan studies. She has lectured and taught also in Australia, Portugal, Greece, and Thailand. Her translations of the poems of Nikos Kavadias won the Columbia University translation prize. She has written extensively on Greek popular music and is currently completing a book on the traditional and contemporary manipulation of grief. Her recent books include *Mauthausen* (translation of a novel by Iakovos Kambanellis), *Dangerous Voices: Women's Laments and Greek Literature*, *Achilles' Fiancee* (translation of a novel by Alki Zei), and *Road to Rembetika: Music of a Greek Sub-Culture* (currently in its fifth edition and available in several translations).

WILLIAM MATTHEWS was the author of more than a dozen books, including eight of original poetry and two of translation. His *Selected Poems & Translations* appeared in 1992. He received fellowships from the National Endowment for the Arts, the John Simon Guggenheim Memorial Foundation, and the Ingram Merrill Foundation; his poetry received the Oscar Blumenthal Award, the Eunice Tietjens Memorial Prize, and the Union League Prize. He taught at Wells College, Cornell University, the Bread Loaf Writers Conference, Columbia University, University of Washington, New York University, City College of New York, and elsewhere. He served on the editorial board of Wesleyan University Press and as poetry editor of *Iowa Review*. He was president of the Poetry Society of America in 1985-89. He died before he could see his translation of *Prometheus Bound* achieve publication.

STEPHEN SANDY graduated from Yale and received his Ph.D. from Harvard University, where he has taught. He has taught also at Tokyo

University, Brown University, the Wesleyan University Writers Conference, the Writing Center at the Chautauqua Institution, and Davidson College. His numerous awards and grants include a National Endowment for the Arts fellowship, an Ingram Merrill Foundation fellowship, a Fulbright Lectureship, the Academy of American Poets Prize, a Dexter Fellowship, Harvard Monthly Prize, Javits Fellowships, and Yaddo residencies. He has been on the faculty of Bennington College since 1969. He is the author of ten books; his *The Thread: New and Selected Poems* has just been published.

DAVID R. SLAVITT was educated at Andover and Yale and has published more than sixty books: original poetry (recently *Eight Longer Poems*), translations (recently *Broken Columns*, of Statius and Claudian), novels (recently *Lives of the Saints*), critical works (recently *Virgil*), and short stories. He worked for seven years as a journalist at *Newsweek* and continues to do freelance reporting and reviewing. With Palmer Bovie he coedited the series Complete Roman Drama in Translation.